"A wonderfully refreshing read that cuts through the slogans and fads to get to the science and substance."
—**JULIA GILLARD**, former Prime Minister of Australia

"[*Don't Be Yourself*] dismantles the authenticity myth through compelling research and insightful analysis. An enlightening read for those ready to evolve."
—**STEFAN SALZER**, Global Head of Human Resources, Red Bull

"With his unique blend of insight and irreverence, Tomas illuminates why we should not chase the illusive and ultimately problematic notion of authenticity but rather cultivate respect, openness, compromise, and commitment to something greater than ourselves. I wish I had written this book!"
—**AMY EDMONDSON**, Novartis Professor of Leadership and Management, Harvard Business School

"If you're tired of cookie-cutter life hacks or leadership advice and ready for something that works in the real world, this entertaining, witty, and authoritative book deserves a prime spot on your desk."
—**ILYA BONIC**, President, Global Career and Head of Strategy, Mercer

"Few books truly challenge the mantras we live by—and this book is one of them. *Don't Be Yourself* reveals the hidden costs of blind authenticity worship and offers a smarter, more socially attuned approach to navigating identity. An eye-opening read."
—**SANDRA MATZ**, author, *Mindmasters: The Data-Driven Science of Predicting and Changing Human Behavior*

"*Don't Be Yourself* is a provocative manifesto for anyone tired of empty workplace mantras. Chamorro-Premuzic doesn't just question the cult of authenticity—he offers a better way to thrive by flexing, editing, and choosing the best version of yourself. This is a timely, necessary book."

—**HERMINIA IBARRA,** Charles Handy Professor of Organizational Behavior, London Business School

"A fascinating and highly readable exploration of the dark side of the advice to 'just be yourself'—and an inspiring manifesto for a more thoughtful, considerate, and effective approach to flourishing at work and in the world at large."

—**OLIVER BURKEMAN,** author, *New York Times* bestseller *Four Thousand Weeks* and *Meditations for Mortals*

"With his signature mix of data and wit, Tomas Chamorro-Premuzic exposes the popular perversion of the lifelong quest to be ourselves and instead proposes changing, performing, and staying close and open to others."

—**GIANPIERO PETRIGLIERI,** Professor of Organizational Behavior, INSEAD

"An intellectually thrilling and morally essential book, *Don't Be Yourself* is a guide to what we're doing wrong—and how to finally get it right. Everyone will benefit from reading this terrific work."

—**JOHANN HARI,** journalist; *New York Times* bestselling author, *Stolen Focus, Chasing the Scream,* and *Lost Connections*

DON'T BE
Yourself

DON'T BE Yourself

Why Authenticity Is Overrated (and What to Do Instead)

TOMAS CHAMORRO-PREMUZIC, PHD

HARVARD BUSINESS REVIEW PRESS
BOSTON, MASSACHUSETTS

Printed in Great Britain

10 9 8 7 6 5 4 3 2

The web addresses referenced in this book were live and correct at the time of the book's publication, but may be subject to change.

Library of Congress Cataloging-in-Publication Data

Names: Chamorro-Premuzic, Tomas author
Title: Don't be yourself : why authenticity is overrated and what to do
    instead / Tomas Chamorro-Premuzic, Ph.D.
Description: Boston, Massachusetts : Harvard Business Review Press, [2025] |
    Includes bibliographical references and index. |
Identifiers: LCCN 2025015525 (print) | LCCN 2025015526 (ebook) |
    ISBN 9781647829834 hardcover | ISBN 9781647829841 epub
Subjects: LCSH: Career development | Authentic leadership |
    Self-realization | Success in business
Classification: LCC HF5381 .C428 2025 (print) | LCC HF5381 (ebook) |
    DDC 650.1—dc23/eng/20250605
LC record available at https://lccn.loc.gov/2025015525
LC ebook record available at https://lccn.loc.gov/2025015526

ISBN: 978-1-64782-983-4
eISBN: 978-1-64782-984-1

To Isabelle and Viktor,
who graciously endure my authentic self—
and wisely know when to edit their own.

"A house that is completely lit up is not livable; likewise, if you are trying to illuminate every single part of you to the world, you are not really worth living with."

—**Werner Herzog**

"Pretending is a very valuable life skill."

—**Meryl Streep**

"You will always be stuck with yourself no matter where you go and what you do."

—**Jarvis Cocker**

"We are what we pretend to be, so we must be careful about what we pretend to be."

—**Kurt Vonnegut**

Contents

DON'T BE Yourself

Authenticity Isn't a Helpful Life Hack

The world worships authenticity—from restaurants offering *real* Mexican, *original* Italian, and *traditional* Chinese food, to ethical baristas grinding single-origin coffee beans, multinational corporations encouraging staff to bring their "whole self to work," and political elections being won or lost largely based on candidates' perceived genuineness, or lack thereof.[1] Whether it's fine art, designer handbags, Hollywood stars, consumer brands, luxury watches, or rare truffles, authenticity augments the value of anything and everything, including humans.[2]

Parents are nagging their children to always be truthful and honest, while children attempt to scrutinize the genuineness of others, whether it's friends, strangers, Santa Claus, the Tooth Fairy, or even their own parents saying that these creatures are real (no spoilers here).[3] Likewise, corporate diversity programs (the *in*effective ones, which means most) nudge women to express their "true selves," and to "just be you," ignoring the wide range of organizational biases and prejudices against them, and the consequences they would face if they actually adhered to these commands—if you need to nudge people to be themselves, you can safely assume they don't feel that it's safe to do so.

Managers and leaders are told to remain uncompromisingly loyal and committed to their own values, and to never yield to any external pressure to act against their own beliefs, whatever these are. This is of course paradoxical, since the pressure on someone to ignore external pressures is both impossible to obey or disobey, like the "don't do what I tell you" command. Furthermore, the only way to succeed by being loyal to your values is to cater to people who share your values in the first place, but this will antagonize everyone else.

Still, we are now so accustomed to the idea that work is an opportunity to find and express our true selves, that we question our jobs and careers when we find ourselves acting in ways that we feel are *not* emblematic of who we "truly are"—or we feel that our work persona is an unnatural or artificial version of ourselves, too distant from our private or personal identity, core values, natural style, and so on. After all, if our full self is not on display at work, our colleagues and bosses may be disinterested in who we really are—how dare they, really!? This explains why, even in relatively stagnant economic environments, workers around the world are quietly quitting their jobs when they don't feel like their "real selves" at work, hoping for a more authentic and magnanimous career path that provides them with a "real purpose," a "true path," or "higher sense of calling."[4] One hundred years ago, it would have been rather odd for a typical assembly line worker to return home after a busy day at the factory and complain to their spouse that, in the past week or so, they "didn't really find a clear sense of purpose," so they should probably quit. Today, this is just ordinary life . . .

Corporate leaders are under public pressure to express their authentic views and core values on polarizing sociopolitical issues, as though their sheer genuineness or openness on these matters could

2

truly shape public perception or solve complex societal challenges. Along the same lines, career consultants, executive coaches, and inspirational TED speakers and gurus are telling us to showcase "who we really are deep down," nudging us to express our authentic thoughts and feelings at work and beyond. For instance, renowned psychologist Brené Brown calls authenticity "the daily practice of letting go of who we think we're supposed to be and embracing who we are."[5] Gabby Bernstein, a bestselling self-help author, notes that "when you are authentic, you create a certain energy, people want to be around you because you are unique."[6] Motivational speaker and leadership guru Robin Sharma argues that "the only way to change the world is to be yourself, because if you try to be anyone else, you'll lose the very essence that makes you unique."[7]

Authenticity is on everybody's mind. Consider that a quick Google Scholar search for academic publications with this keyword produces over one million hits for the last five years alone. To put this into perspective, that's twice as many as for *happiness, stress,* or *Covid-19,* and fifty times more than for *career success.* In 2023, *authenticity* was chosen as word of year by the Merriam Webster dictionary, a decision the editors justified by the fact that, like no other concept, authenticity cuts across stories and conversations about artificial intelligence (AI), celebrity culture, identity, and social media.[8]

Authenticity shines bright and strong like our moral North Star, promising to guide us in our path to a more prosperous, healthy, and happy living. Indeed, the rallying cry for authenticity has become virtually unassailable. And yet, the popularity of an idea has never been a reliable indicator of its utility, logic, or truth. Whether it's believing lightning never strikes twice in the same place (it frequently does, and multiple times), that humans only use 10 percent of their brain (actually, we use nearly 100 percent of our brain every day, though not necessarily at the same time), that the Great Wall of China is the only human-made object visible from space (in fact, it usually isn't visible from space, unlike, say, large airports), or that the earth is flat (hopefully no explanation is needed here), there is no shortage of widely endorsed misconceptions about the world. As Oscar Wilde famously noted in *The Picture of Dorian Gray*, more often than not, the wisdom of the crowds is more like the exact reverse, such that "everything popular is wrong."[9]

To be sure, debunking myths and misconceptions—that have been cemented over time to become almost convictions for the vast majority of people—takes a superlative amount of time and effort, as well as a great deal of research, evidence, and facts. And even then, there's no guarantee you will convince others to change their minds, since it is all too easy to dismiss unwanted facts and unpopular truths. As Jonathan Swift noted, "Falsehood flies, and the truth comes limping after it" (fittingly, a paraphrased version of this quote is usually misattributed to Mark Twain).[10]

What if our collective obsession with authenticity—this relentless pursuit of being true to ourselves—was deeply flawed? What if the very concept of authenticity, as we currently understand it, was misguided at best and harmful at worst? What if chasing authenticity was an actual trap—one that oversimplifies human complexity, disregards the necessity of compromise, and leaves us ill-equipped to navigate the nuanced realities of modern life, which include focusing not just on ourselves and how we feel, but also on others?

The Perils of Authenticity

In my thirty-year career as a psychologist, I have always been fascinated—and at times also disturbed—by the gap between scientific research and popular beliefs about human behavior. This fascination led me to research and publish books on the downsides of confidence (as well as the upsides of moderate insecurities and, even, imposter syndrome), the troublesome gap between the leaders we need and those we actually get (which explains why so many incompetent men become leaders), and the alarming impact of AI on human behavior (including its ability to turn us into a more impulsive, impatient, narrow-minded, and boring version of ourselves).[11]

My approach here is generally the same, namely, to use data and science to refine oversimplified popular narratives and opinions on important career, work, and organizational issues into more nuanced, evidence-based, and accurate knowledge, thus replacing popular misconceptions with facts and reason. Because, as Daniel Boorstin noted, "The biggest enemy of knowledge is not ignorance, but the illusion of knowledge."[12]

No topic better illustrates this disconnect—between what we believe and what science says about human behavior—than authenticity. Indeed, few psychological traits are more frequently touted as desirable, moral, and socially advantageous than authenticity, with millions of blogs, books, and articles dedicated to its benefits. We appear to have turned pure, unfiltered personal expression into an ultimate life hack, a moral and noble goal in itself, with no regard for what truly drives effective interpersonal functioning in any meaningful interaction, particularly in consequential settings such as work.

To some, my contrarian view may seem controversial. After I told a colleague that I was intending to write a critique of the authenticity cult, his response was that it may even be easier to take down Taylor Swift (which, incidentally, should not be dismissed purely on the basis of her popularity and cachet, so perhaps not a bad idea for my next book).

My aim isn't to take shots at our current views about authenticity just for the sake of being controversial or polemical. Nor am I trying to deny some of the personal advantages of authenticity, which partly explain its popularity. Notably, research has repeatedly highlighted the many benefits of *subjective* authenticity, in the sense of *feeling* that you are acting in accordance with your true or real self, as opposed to external pressures or extrinsic forces (e.g., etiquette, culture, authority, and social norms). Since the rise of positive psychology in the 1970s, many positive correlations between this subjective dimension of authenticity on the one hand, and a range of desirable and valuable work and real-life outcomes on the other, have been identified and replicated.[13]

For instance, empirical studies show that people who report experiencing a more authentic self are also more likely to report higher levels of job, career, and relationship satisfaction.[14] In other words, when we feel more authentic, we also tend to experience more positive moods and self-views, as well as higher levels of confidence, and we are more likely to display a stronger teamwork orientation and a higher levels of work performance.[15] Authenticity has also been linked to higher levels of subjective well-being, with some studies pointing to a causal connection, such that feeling more authentic would result in higher levels of happiness, life satisfaction, and psychological well-being.[16] The benefits of subjective authenticity also appear to extend beyond the workplace. In the realm of love and relationships, studies show that perceiving your romantic partner as authentic is associated with higher marital satisfaction, though the causal direction isn't clear (one would expect relationship satisfaction to boost the feeling that your partner is being authentic).[17] Feeling authentic also produces a sense of subjective positivity that tends to reduce the likelihood that you behave aggressively toward others, whether they are strangers or friends.[18]

But the existing research on authenticity reveals a fundamental challenge. Despite widespread enthusiasm, the term remains frustratingly elusive, ambiguous, and contradictory. Whether it applies to brands, organizations, art, or humans, authenticity means different things to different people—with the notable exception that, whatever it means, it is implied that it should mean something positive, and that authenticity is an experience we should all cherish and try to pursue.[19]

In fact, the popular "just be yourself" advice that underpins the mainstream authenticity cult is in stark contrast with the extensive scientific evidence on the major determinants of career success, leadership effectiveness, and effective diversity and inclusion interventions. As this book will illustrate, even if such advice is well-intended, it is likely to backfire, straining our relationships and stalling our career growth, not to mention handicapping our image and brand in professional and career settings.

In particular, popular assumptions about authenticity are completely at odds with what well-adjusted and functioning humans and emotionally mature adults must do if they are interested in having successful interactions with others, and harnessing a positive reputation at work and beyond.[20] Whatever you may hear about the virtues of authenticity and "just being yourself," the fact of the matter is that most people work in teams and organizations that actually reward strategic self-presentation (the intentional act of putting on a carefully rehearsed and choreographed professional self, especially so it comes across as genuine) over unfiltered self-expression (especially if it's not prosocial or professional). And, like most people, your current and future colleagues, coworkers, and bosses will appreciate seeing and interacting with your professional rather than your uninhibited self. They will also be grateful for your efforts to display your *best* rather than your "real" or "whole" self.

Furthermore, even when we *feel* more "authentic" and experience some subjective comfort from identifying with our actions, there's absolutely no guarantee that others will feel the same way. What's good for us may not be good for others, which is a problem because our career advancement, and pretty much any objective aspiration we may have in any area of life, is dependent on how *others* perceive us (rather than how we perceive or feel about ourselves). Contrary to what the authenticity cult predicates, success is rarely attained through radical honesty or by always showing every single side of ourselves. Instead, it's a function of carefully managing your self-presentation—adapting to situations and showcasing the qualities that are best appreciated by others—while making an effort to conceal negative, undesirable, and irrelevant aspects of your personality.

The most successful people aren't brutally honest, uncomfortably transparent, or intensely authentic. Rather, they are masters at reading a room, adapting their approach, and showcasing precisely the qualities that will resonate with a particular audience at precisely the right moment. They know when to dial up certain traits and when to dial down others. They are able to draw from a very wide behavioral repertoire that enables them to respond flexibly and effectively to each situation, without coming across as fake or dishonest. As this book will attempt to show, all of this requires a great deal of effort, practice, and paying attention to how our behavior impacts others, rather than expecting others to adjust or adapt to our natural or spontaneous self.

Though rarely discussed, there's a well-established body of research on the counterproductive and antisocial elements of authenticity, particularly when those individuals who feel they can "just be themselves" are occupying positions of power, status, or leadership. This research is best understood within the wider cultural zeitgeist of rampant individualism and egotistical self-absorption that characterizes our times—a zeitgeist that puts individuals on a pedestal, even when those who succeed do so at the expense of bullying, belittling, or manipulating others, and even when those individuals who are celebrated as role models for their personal success have a catastrophic effect on their teams, organizations, and societies at large.[21] This narcissistic zeitgeist elevates self-expression above all else, worshipping self-belief while undermining self-development. In this way, the authenticity narrative may have started as a well-intended call for honesty, but, alas, digressed or morphed into a justification for and celebration of egotism and entitlement, wielding authenticity as a shield against constructive feedback and a license to prioritize personal feelings over shared goals or communal interests. It is, to put it plainly, as if the freedom to be ourselves had completely nullified our obligation to others . . .

Entitlement and narcissism have been increasing for generations, so it should come as no surprise that the "just be yourself" mantra—which prompts us to disregard what other people think of us and assume that if we think we are special, then we actually are—has become not just a normalized tenet of our social etiquette, but a widely adored and celebrated moral ideal.[22] So much so, that suggestions that it may be worth editing our unfiltered thoughts or at least taming our obnoxious habits may be seen as ludicrous, insane, or heretic (even if such suggestions are actually authentic). Same goes for the notion that it could be beneficial to question or scrutinize our values now and then, as opposed to just blindly following them, as though we were a possessed member of a cult—the cult of *me*.

As this book will illustrate, the more effort we invest in *not* being our spontaneous, natural, or unfiltered selves, the better the version of ourselves we can present to others and the world. This deliberate approach to cultivating and harnessing the best version of ourselves not only increases our chances of achieving meaningful and tangible success—both in the short and long term—but also aligns us with external benchmarks of excellence, rather than limiting us to our own subjective, overly forgiving self-assessments.[23] Authenticity may be an appealing feeling and could be sold as inherently virtuous, but it is usually through transcending our natural instincts and cultivating new adaptations (especially when it means going beyond our default habits and learning to go against our nature) that we can forge better connections with others and become a better version of ourselves.

Part One

HOW AUTHENTICITY HURTS US

1

The Four
Authenticity Traps

Despite the nebulous, wishy-washy nature of the "authenticity" concept, there are some generally agreed-upon attributes or definitional foundations for the term, which highlight some of its most commonly associated qualities, especially in mainstream or popular uses.

Most notably, authenticity entails *genuineness* (being truthful to others and yourself), *congruence* (acting in line with your values), and *autonomy* (ignoring external pressures so as to behave freely). It also concerns the imperative of blending our personal and professional selves by "bringing our whole self to work" or eliminating the psychological distance between our work and our personal identity.

In other words, authenticity tends to denote transparency, consistency, and commitment to one's "true" values and behaviors, and it also showcases these attributes in work environments in the hope of reducing the differences between our work and non-work personas. Along these lines, the authenticity movement propels us to express and showcase our unfiltered self regardless of the situation, to commit to making no compromises, to never yield to external pressures to tame or inhibit our personal self, and to never act out of character or in conflict with our values.

Even if these tenets are promoted in good spirit, they are likely to, at best, create a fair amount of psychological confusion in those who attempt to follow them. At worst, they will propel people to counter-productive, maladaptive, and unwise behaviors and decisions. A proper examination of these tenets—against both the science of ef-fective interpersonal skills and the wider range of rules governing desirable norms and behavioral etiquette in any given culture—suggests that authenticity is not just naive, but also inauthentic as a formula for improving people's career and life success.

The basic tenets of authenticity are better seen as factoids, in the sense that they are more like urban legends or refutable myths than concrete truths. Perhaps more worryingly, these principles result in a series of problematic *traps* that inhibit our ability to behave in proso-cial or effective ways with others, not to mention our ability to un-derstand the demands of each situation.

Trap 1: Always Be Honest, with Yourself and Others

This first authenticity trap has become something of a universal moral, and its message is embodied by the positive psychology notion that authenticity involves "the reduction of phoniness toward the zero point." In essence, this principle champions truthfulness with ourselves and others, and refraining from being a fake or a fraud.

In the inspirational words of Oprah: "You can run away from your-self for a very long time. You can be married to the wrong person for decades and pretend it's fine. You can fake it doing work you only half care about. You can hide behind accoutrements, square footage, and cars. Big-screen TVs and fancy vacations. But you will never get away with being a phony." Who can argue with this? As a matter of fact, in addition to the mega-successful Oprah, every religion, moral code, cultural etiquette, and parenting philosophy values truth over lies and knowledge over ignorance, not to mention good faith over bad faith.

And yet, when we look at the more practical and mundane realities of real-world interactions, particularly those considered prosocial rather than antisocial or toxic, there are many caveats and nuances to the seemingly unquestionable notion that truth is always preferable to the alternatives, especially when we prioritize not just our own self-interest, but also the interest of others. A simple cost-benefit analysis at the individual level indicates that there are not only some clear benefits to offering a diluted and edited version of honesty or truth to others, but also significant benefits to not being honest with ourselves.[1]

For starters, it is hard to be truthful to yourself unless you know yourself really well in the first place. As it turns out, to truly know yourself, you may need to undergo years of psychotherapy, make strong advances in mindfulness and meditation, find yourself in an Indian ashram, or experiment with psychedelics, all of which can be time-consuming and tedious if you don't really gravitate toward these activities or have time to spare—oh, and there is no guarantee you will *actually* truly know yourself, so the reward is uncertain. At best, you may convince yourself that you have found yourself or a different version of yourself, but there's no objective way to actually verify this. As many eminent figures across these and other disciplines have noted, the important part is the journey rather than the destination, not least because you will never truly find yourself or discover "who you really are." In the best of cases, you will just find a less-distorted story about yourself and your identity than others may have about theirs. For Freud, who devoted more thought than anyone else to finding his and everybody else's "real" self, there were just two possible outcomes for this journey—realizing that there is no answer (meaning you are *neurotic*, which is code for being insecure and a perpetual prisoner of your ruminations and anxieties), which is the best option, or embracing a wrong answer with delusional conviction (meaning you are *psychotic*, which is code for being totally detached from reality), which is the worst option.

Coming to terms with uncomfortable aspects of your character and personality, and seeing yourself as others see you (especially outside the small circle of people who love you or at least have learned to put up with you) can be traumatic—there's a reason why "depressive realist" is the psychological term for the minority of people blessed with the capacity for self-awareness and an ability to make accurate interpretations of reality. In contrast, distorting reality in your favor, and seeing yourself in a self-serving, self-enhancing, and overly optimistic manner is comforting, and may even have a contagious effect on others.

As chapter 2 will illustrate, there is a good explanation for the common human tendency to engage in self-deceptive and self-delusional thinking, particularly if you want *others* to see you as authentic. For instance, you may disagree with President Donald Trump when he claims that he is a "stable genius," but the fact that he appears to genuinely believe this makes him seem rather authentic, as well as making others more likely to believe him (it is a lot easier to fool other people after you have already fooled yourself). And, in an age where a large portion of the general public has become quite cynical of politicians, there is no shortage of people who would rather vote for a politician who appears to say what they truly think (like Trump), even if said voters don't agree, than for a politician who appears to tell voters what they may want to hear. Ironically, telling people something that seems incredible, unusual, disruptive of the status quo, and even incompatible with their beliefs may convince them that you are brave and courageous for telling the truth—in other words, authentic.

More obvious perhaps, regardless of whether you are truthful to yourself or not, are the many practical advantages of *not* telling others what you think or feel all the time, and to prioritizing *their* thoughts and feelings (rather than yours) when you interact with them. For example, between someone who is honest but rude, and someone who is fake but kind, the latter will succeed far more frequently, especially if they are able to combine their false kindness with social skills, including good acting skills. In fact, people are so interested in being liked and appreciated that it's often unnecessary to master impression management (i.e., the art of performative acting in the service of creating a positive or desirable image with others) as an effective alternative to honesty, because the self-serving tendency for people to hear what they want to hear and see what they want to see is more or less ubiquitous. So even if you are making neutral remarks about others, they will likely interpret them as flattery or compliments. And yet it is surprising how often we decide to go to great lengths to give others a piece of our mind and ensure that they are fully aware of our negative opinions and feelings, just because we assume that expressing our authentic views must be prioritized. In fact, a much better suggestion to the "always be truthful with others" trap would be to "make an effort to be kind and act like you genuinely mean it."

Trap 2: Follow Your Heart and Be True to Your Values

In essence, this trap encourages us to act according to our instincts, spontaneous feelings, or inner moral compass (the "heart" part), and to refrain from making compromises between what we feel is right on the one hand, and the pressures of external demands, societal rules, or outside moral imperatives on the other. For instance, if I think someone has done something that, according to my own moral compass, is wrong, I should assume that they are wrong and I am right, end of story. And if someone believes something that is incompatible with my belief system or acts in ways that are incongruent with my values, I should rightly assume they are misguided, confused, or wrong, if not all three together. Even when people tell me that I acted the wrong way, I should not be bothered by this, so long as I feel that I acted the right way, and so on. In short, my thoughts, feelings, and actions ought to be judged only according to my own core beliefs and values, rather than those of others.

Two interconnected assumptions underpin this rule. First, that the ultimate yardstick guiding our actions is whatever *we* feel is right. In other words, there can be no unethical or wrong decision if we are truly listening to our heart. Second, that our intuitive or spontaneous feelings and emotions carry more wisdom than logic or reason ever could.

Rather romantically, then, we ought to let ourselves go, so as to be fearlessly guided by our passions and desires, and the truth will set us free. It is through this act that our real self will emerge. Anything else will likely turn us into a fraud or imposter living a fake and meaningless existence. As you can see, this rule aligns with the first authenticity trap, in the sense that being true to your values reinforces the notion that you ought to be honest with yourself.

Again, the instruction to just follow your heart may feel intuitively right, as well as morally laudable. Except . . . intuitions are *feelings* about facts, rather than actual facts—after all, our intuition tends to tell us that our intuition is right! Now, I'm not sure what your specific principles are, but I suspect you will not be surprised to hear that they are not necessarily shared by everyone else. And, while everyone has

18

their own values, some values are generally better than others, at least when judged from an impartial and objective vantage point (such as how those values impact other people, rather than yourself).[2]

Consider all the suffering caused in the world—I'm talking about human-induced harm at scale, rather than, say, natural deaths, tornadoes, or shark attacks, which kill and injure far fewer humans than humans do intentionally. For instance, when we look at destructive dictatorships, civil wars, corrupt governments, incompetent rulers, failed states, collapsed institutions, toxic managers and organizations, and the unquantifiable number of racist, sexist, prejudiced, aggressive, and antisocial acts that cause so much suffering in the world, it would no doubt be of some comfort to attribute these nasty things to people who are simply failing to follow their values or listen to their hearts. However, it is largely the inverse, where such people have no reservations following their crooked, corrupt, or counterproductive values (as opposed to censoring and overhauling them with societal values that are more prosocial and benevolent to *most*, even if they come at the expense of personal or individual gains).[3]

And if you find these examples too extreme, then consider a milder version. Namely, the fact that we are increasingly polarized and divided at work because of our inability to make compromises allowing us to respect or tolerate, let alone love, people whose values are markedly different from ours, and the fact that only hate seems to unite us these days, in the sense that people who share a hatred of others with different values are themselves united. When this egocentric self-radicalization of beliefs and attitudes turns our values into a rigid system that fuels antisocial intolerance, asking us to be true to them is like throwing gasoline on the fire.

Most of the individuals who have detrimental effects on others and society (including corrosive, parasitic, or toxic effects on workplace cultures) tend to act in accordance with their own moral code—

which just happens to be flawed, in the sense that they have little empathic concern for others, and pursue a selfish agenda above all. More often than not, they will even rationalize and justify their behavior as perfectly moral, to the point of regarding themselves as ethical referents or moral bastions of society, at least in their imaginary version. When they follow their heart rather than their mind, the latter goes along with a thumbs up, to everyone else's peril.[4]

So perhaps the "be true to your values" mantra should be recommended only to those who have the *right*, or at least benevolent, values to begin with. Except this would open a can of worms—how can we judge whether someone's values are acceptable or not, without indulging in some form of self-centered or righteous moral ethnocentrism? Note that a great deal of harm in the world has been caused by the moral repression or oppression of other people's values, especially when done in the name of values that are (at times unintentionally) wrong, harmful, or antisocial.[5]

By the same token, organizations may be inclined to suppress or censor certain individual values under the conviction that *their* organizational values, namely the values of the majority, elite, or status quo, should dominate and even eclipse contrarian beliefs. Historical and present examples of how this unfolds abound, from organizations antagonizing discrepant individual beliefs on gender equality vs. inequality, meritocracy vs. nepotism, or freedom of thought vs. social harmony.[6]

To be sure, the moral or immoral nature of convictions is often dependent on time and wider historical events. By today's standards, the common behavioral etiquette of most corporate cultures in the 1960s would be considered racist and sexist (though undoubtedly some people are somewhat nostalgic of them), which suggests that progress and evolution bring about important upgrades in civility and prosocial behaviors. This also suggests that, by standards that will exist in, say, the 2060s, some of the things we deem acceptable and morally sound today will (hopefully) be considered prejudiced and discriminatory then, such that our cultural evolution will continue—but we won't know how it will evolve until we get there, or in what precise direction.

Even leaving morality aside, the "follow your heart" mantra introduces a wide range of other complications. Letting go of our inhibitions, ignoring our "super-ego," and following our passions—basically, going with the flow or letting ourselves be driven by our instincts or intuition—can be both self-destructive and destructive to others. Unless you are a Buddhist monk, you will have firsthand experience of the thin line between "letting loose" and "losing control," whether it involves our lifestyle habits, exchanges with others, or career-related ambitions. In the battle between heart and mind, logic drafts the strategy, but emotion storms the battlefield, often burning the map in the process. Humans are perfectly capable of acting rationally, but we mostly behave in predictably irrational ways, precisely because we prefer to go with the flow and follow our heart rather than logic.

Most of the poor decisions we make in life—as well as our prejudices, biases, self-destructive tendencies, poor habits, impulsivities, and immature reactions—are all consequences of following our emotions rather than reason (*thinking fast*, which is a euphemism for, well, not thinking at all).[7] The world would be a much better place if we learned or at least tried to resist our passions, distrust our intuition, and tame our instincts (including our capacity to question and distrust rather than blindly follow our values). Granted, this would perhaps also be a more boring world, but levels of suffering would arguably decrease. People would be less polarized and tribal. They would be more open to understanding and accepting each other's points of view, particularly when they are not like each other. And they would be better able to control the self-handicapping behaviors they wished they didn't exhibit, such as escalating work conflicts, offending colleagues, and crossing their bosses with an excess of spontaneous truth.

Needless to say, controlling our spontaneous reactions and increasing our ability to *not* follow our passions and emotions would also reduce the amount of prejudice and discrimination that exists in the world, as we would all be less likely to pre-judge, more likely to have an open mind *and* heart, and more likely to rethink issues from other people's point of view. Furthermore, we would also be much better at showing restraint and exercising self-control. The reason why 80 percent of New Year's resolutions are broken within a few months, and then largely recycled in following years (albeit not without guilt), is that it's all too easy to be guided by our habits, passions, and default character traits.[8]

Likewise, most of the relationship, work, and interpersonal conflicts in the world are caused by us expecting *other* people to change, which is a perfect excuse for remaining unchanged ourselves, and "just going with the flow." Everybody loves change until they have to do it themselves. In an ideal world, we would remain unchanged, while everyone else changes in our direction instead, like celestial bodies adjusting their orbits to accommodate our fixed position at the center, as if we were the sun and they were mere planets, moons, or passing asteroids, dutifully revolving around our gravitational special self! Unfortunately, this is also what others expect of us. The end result is a world in which most people are stubbornly convinced that they are right and others are wrong, and that the world—and particularly the humans that inhabit it—must revolve around them.[9]

Trap 3: Stop Worrying About What Others Think of You

In a world saturated with opinions, from social media "likes" to workplace feedback, there's something seductive about imagining yourself as impervious to it all, operating with complete autonomy and self-assurance. It's hard to deny the romantic appeal of this idea. The notion of liberating yourself from the judgment of others carries an almost mythic quality, and suggests a path to authenticity, self-confidence, and unshakable inner peace. One can almost taste the freedom.

But here's the catch: Completely ignoring what others think isn't just unrealistic, it's counterproductive as well (or it *would be*, if we could ever achieve it). As social beings, our relationships, reputations, and successes are deeply interconnected with the perceptions of others. Feedback from others is not a curse, but the essential ingredient for self-awareness, not to mention critical for our growth and self-improvement, particularly when it highlights an uncomfortable gap between the person we want to be and how others see us. It is only by paying attention to others that we can get a sense of what others think of us, which is critical information if we want to avoid an unrealistic sense of self or utter delusion. In the famous words of Charles Horton Cooley, "I am not what I think I am, and I am not what you think I am. I am what I think you think I am."[10] Because, in most situations, other people—our bosses, our bosses' bosses, our colleagues, and even our friends and acquaintances—are the ones who enable and determine our options for growth and career success, by either opening or closing doors; so it would be foolish to ignore what they think of us. You may be tempted to think that you're killing it, but if everyone else thinks you're an idiot, your obliviousness is going to hurt your career, whether you are aware of it or not. Incidentally, when others are of the opinion that you suck, *and* that you are totally unaware of the fact that you suck, they will think even more poorly of you.

Importantly, you don't stop caring about others' opinions simply because you love yourself; you stop caring when self-love turns into a narcissistic or entitled self-obsession, blinding you from reality and making you a hero in your own mind—a solipsistic narcissist.[11] In that sense, you may love yourself *because* you stop caring about others' opinions, but that kind of self-love is maladaptive, delusional, and antisocial, not to mention short-lived, because it disconnects you from others. As in the original myth of *Narcissus,* you end up drowning in your own self-love.

It is not the honest pursuit of mastery (e.g., skills, talents, success, and accomplishments), but rather delusional egomania, that makes people ignore others' views of them. As a matter of fact, those who acquire true mastery do so through repeatedly *attending* to, rather than ignoring, others' opinions of them, especially when those others have the necessary expertise and honesty to provide them with critical feedback. In the end, everything we think, believe, and feel has been shaped by other people. Nothing is ever fully our own idea, thought, or creation; and even our deepest convictions and our personal moral compass have been transmitted—if not inculcated—to us by others.

Whether we try to do X or *not* do X, we are still influenced by X. We are not just defined by what we love, but also by what we hate or negate. Whether we are conscious of it or not, moving toward an action is always a way of moving away from another, and doing something is always also a way of *not* doing something else. So, while it sounds romantic to develop a sense of indifference to others, the reality is that we cannot exist (let alone think, learn, or develop) while being truly immune to the influence of other people. So much so, that even in total isolation, we will continue to be influenced by the memory or thought of other people (for Tom Hanks's character in *Cast Away*, Wilson was not just a volleyball, but also a companion), and by everything we have internalized from our significant others.

Needless to say, the command to ignore what others say is a logical paradox or impossibility, because if we truly wanted to follow it, we would need to ignore that command, too, and if we wanted to ignore it, we would actually end up following it—just like the "don't do what I tell you" advice.

Trap 4: Bring Your Whole Self to Work

According to TED speaker and consultant Mike Robbins, this trap entails "fully showing up" and "allowing ourselves to be truly seen" by our coworkers, without hiding any elements of our character, personality, or identity, for we should not conceal any thoughts, emotions, or attitudes due to shame or embarrassment, but rather quite the opposite.

In simple terms, this implies that our colleagues, bosses, employees, and coworkers are not just interested in interacting with our professional self or work persona, but also eager to know the "full breadth and depth" of our character and identity—including our personal or private self, which comprises all our beliefs, opinions, and preferences, irrespective of how unrelated they are to work. Strictly speaking, bringing your whole self to work implies that there is simply no aspect of you that is not relevant or welcome at work; you must display the totality of yourself without disguising anything, as every aspect of you is to be celebrated by others at work.

In line with this implication, some of the world's most successful and recognizable corporations (including Netflix, Deloitte, Bain &

25

Co, LinkedIn, Airbnb, and Google) invite employees and job seekers to bring their whole self to work. This trend suggests that if we ever find ourselves in a job where this is not encouraged—where we had to somehow mask any aspects of our identity (including our sexual preferences, favorite pastimes, secret hobbies, childhood fears, adult anxieties, political convictions, guilty pleasures, and not to mention our unconventional attitudes and wacky beliefs)—then it would be safe to assume that we are not in the right job or organization and that we must find a job somewhere else, where our nonprofessional self may feel welcome and experience a strong sense of belonging.

To be sure, there's some logic to this idea, supported by empirical evidence that people on average do enjoy their jobs more when they *identify* with their work persona. This idea was pioneered by William Kahn, who coined the term "employee engagement" back in 1990, and postulated that when people feel a close psychological connection with their work persona—in the sense of seeing it as something that fits in nicely or blends in well with their personal identity, or is seamlessly integrated with their personal character traits—they will be significantly more energized and motivated by work rather than when they see their work persona as alien (which is of course alienating).[12] However, there is a big difference between that and actually bringing your whole self to work, which involves inviting all dimensions of yourself—including those usually considered private and personal—to your office, a client's office, or an online office space, such as Zoom.

For starters, as the Italian entrepreneur and thought-leader Riccarda Zezza notes, our self-concept is typically too complex and wide-ranging to be restricted or limited to our professional self or work persona. Indeed, most of us inhabit multiple selves, such that our character and identity is multidimensional, encompassing a range of roles (e.g., husband, wife, father, mother, brother, sister, son, daughter, friend, and captain of the volleyball team) that may or may not have much to do with our work persona.[13] At times, there are useful adjacencies and commonalities between some of these roles—parenting skills could be useful for managing people, and being the captain of your sports team can help you develop your leadership skills—but this doesn't mean we should bring all the dimensions of our self to work or express the bits that aren't relevant.

While organizations may encourage us to behave at work in ways that are congruent with these non-professional roles—and to perhaps even share some stories or experiences about these roles with our work colleagues, in the spirit of bonding or connecting with them—we are not evaluated, rewarded, hired, or promoted for bringing our whole self to work. If we were, then we would rightly expect our personal and extraprofessional activities to compensate for our poor work performance.

For instance, when our manager complains that we didn't hit our work goals, or that our productivity is lagging, we may respond that they shouldn't worry, because we have otherwise been a great spouse or wonderful parent, and we enjoy the fact that our job does not interfere with that. Or we might respond that, in the past weeks, we were busy helping our colleague get over their divorce, prioritized keeping up with the latest political news, or were simply captivated by an array of interesting YouTube videos at work, all of which may have, alas, interfered with the formal aspects of our job performance, including our key work objectives. Nonetheless, we still clearly deserve our manager's recognition and praise, as we didn't keep any important personal aspects of our personal self disconnected from work. Rather, we were just busy catering to most other aspects of our whole self.

Incidentally, it is worth noting that our whole self also comprises the moody, argumentative, opinionated, and immature elements of our personality, so one would also expect the companies that advocate for bringing the whole self to also reward us for expressing these rather undesirable and probably objectionable character traits at work and unleashing them onto our colleagues. Of course, the same goes for our colleagues as well. So, when your obnoxious coworkers irritate you, just be happy about the fact that they are bringing their whole self to work, as opposed to holding back or editing themselves just to spare you. Same for when they express a blatant bias against your views, opinions, and thoughts. You should be delighted that they have chosen to be so genuine, and refrained from leaving their opinionated and biased selves at home. And even when they decide to engage in bullying, harassment, or abuse—how lucky we are that they are bringing their whole self to work!

When we decide to express our personal preferences and beliefs (including our sexual orientations, political affiliations, religious views, and ideological convictions), it is one thing to be encouraged to express them, and quite another to have them accepted, let alone celebrated. For example, when you visit someone's house and the host insists that you don't need to take your shoes off, while everybody else (including the host) does—it is not really a sincere statement, but rather an educated or polite way of letting you figure out on your own that you really ought to take them off. Moreover, even if the invitation to bring your whole self to work was truly sincere, we should not necessarily assume that employees have a genuine desire to blend their personal or private self with their professional or work persona, or to reveal their intimate views, feelings, or preferences to their colleagues, and so on.

It may also be worth specifying whether the "bring your whole self to work" mantra is really a blanket invitation to express your personal self, or whether it is constrained to those attitudes, beliefs, and preferences that happen to match existing cultural norms, such that it is not free of guardrails. If we truly valued diversity and wanted to encourage every employee to express their unique personal identity in an uncensored and uninhibited way, we may need to think not just about allowing them to express the specific preferences that happen to be acceptable or en vogue with top management, or the majority of the workforce, but also the exact reverse. For instance, it would not suffice to invite people to report that they are gay or straight, but also that they are homophobic or heterophobic. By the same token, the invitation ought to be extended not just to liberals and conservatives, but also fascists, right wing fundamentalists, holocaust deniers, and racists. After all, why be a racist only in your private life, when you can bring your uninhibited racist self to the office, as encouraged by the policy?

It is also noteworthy that, even if bringing your whole self to work makes you enjoy your job more—and assuming it doesn't make others enjoy their job less—there is only a weak correlation (less than 10 percent overlap) between enjoying your job and actually being good at it. And besides, bringing your whole self to work is by no means a prerequisite for enjoying your job in the first place.[14]

Many people are much happier maintaining a distance between their professional and personal self, and especially keeping their private thoughts, beliefs, and preferences, well, private! This is usually for a good reason: Even when organizations pretend to reward authenticity, what they actually reward is *culture fit*, which involves behaving in ways that are seen as appropriate and congruent with how things are done around an organization.[15] Despite good intentions, organizational cultures, like any group of people, are optimized for blending in and following process and norms. For every cultural misfit, there must be many more people who fit in, so as to make work predictable and allow for the coordination of individual employee behaviors so that they can become a well-oiled unit and a high-performing team.[16] This doesn't mean becoming an automaton or erasing your individuality; it just means the priority is to adjust to a collective optimum, so that everyone can focus on adding value to the team and organization, as opposed to expressing their individual needs. If leadership is the art of building high-performing teams, it is mostly a function of persuading people to temporarily set aside their selfish or individualistic agendas, so they can collaborate effectively and become a valuable team member.[17]

To be sure, some people are given license to challenge, and even disrupt, the existing culture and norms of a group, but they first need to fit in and persuade others, especially the status quo, that their intentions are good, they possess the capabilities (e.g., talents, skills, potential, etc.) for reshaping the dominant norms, and they are worthy of an exceptional license to operate outside the rules of the game. It is the same with elite athletes in top professional teams: Before they stand out or impose their own style and influence on the team (hopefully with the goal of improving it), their performance must be optimized by fitting in and becoming a valuable team member. Once you convince people that you are great at playing the game with the existing rules, you will be given some license to change the rules.

This works in exactly the same way when we look at corporate teams and social communities: Unless you persuade others that you are unusually talented, or capable of operating effectively as a leader, you are better off fitting in and contributing as a team player, rather than being desperately focused on standing out. In order to cooperate and collaborate effectively with others, we must all adhere to some norms and rules, which, more often than not, will call for leaving some parts of our individual, private, and personal identity at home. In fact, if we want an inclusive organizational culture, as well as effective teams that leverage their diversity in order to work well together, we must each set aside some of our individual qualities in order to function as a cohesive team unit. This will build trust and unity in the team, and allow it to focus on what truly matters (i.e., results), rather than the satisfaction or fulfillment of individual members.

As the next chapters will show, the four authenticity traps discussed above share one important commonality: While positioned as important lubricants of personal success and interpersonal effectiveness, they may oftentimes self-handicap or inhibit people's performance and harm their reputation. Indeed, it is precisely in the very contexts in which authenticity is most heavily promoted that it actually tends to backfire—whether as a career strategy, a path to fairness, or a tool for upgrading our relationships.

As the rest of this book will attempt to highlight, the evidence points to a counterintuitive conclusion: The advice to "not be yourself" is actually more likely to lead to success. Let us dig deeper into each of the four traps in order to explain this further.

2

Trap 1

Always Be Honest,
with Yourself and Others

The most obvious meanings associated with authenticity are genuineness, sincerity, and honesty, especially in interpersonal relationships. An authentic person, in this sense, is truthful with others, as opposed to someone who deceives or cheats.[1] As simple as this may sound, there are two problems with this idea.

The first is that people are hardly ever true to themselves, which obviously makes it difficult for them to be truthful with others.[2] For example, if you ask me whether I ate the last cookie and I answer "no,"—not because I haven't, but because I mistakenly *think* I haven't (perhaps I forgot, or I erroneously assumed it wasn't the last one)—it would be hard to interpret my answer as truthful. However, it could still be considered genuine or authentic in that it expresses my honest view or opinion on the matter. Likewise, when an employee challenges their boss over a negative performance review, the issue may not lie in the inaccuracy of the review, but in the employee's overinflated self-view—same for a student challenging their teacher over a low grade. Similarly, when we ask people whether they are a "nice person"—most people truly believe that they are, so they answer "yes," but this doesn't make their answers automatically truthful, even if they are authentic.

To complicate matters further, we are far more likely to persuade others that we did not eat the cookie or that we excelled in our job if we've already convinced (euphemism for "bullsh--ted") ourselves. This is why there are advantages to *not* being truthful to ourselves, and why self-deception is far more prevalent than self-awareness, and not just in political leaders: Fool yourself first, and you will more easily fool others, as self-deception is often a self-fulfilling prophecy that frequently upgrades to *other*-deception—and with marvelous personal results, at least while it lasts.[3] Conversely, if we lack the ability to fool ourselves, our attempts to deny eating the last cookie or underperforming at work are more likely to falter, for our performance will be unconvincing. Like self-deception, self-doubt is contagious as well. Therefore, if we want to be truthful to others, we are left with two suboptimal choices: Confess and own our mistakes, which is akin to hanging ourselves; or deliver a nervous performance riddled with anxiety, insecurity, and a fear of being found out. Oh, and whatever choice we make, our competition will consist largely of people who are much more effective at bullsh--ting others because they have already bullsh--ted themselves . . .

Needless to say, self-deception can be strategically used for ill intentions. Although we will never know for sure, it is plausible that George W. Bush and Tony Blair truly believed that Saddam Hussein possessed weapons of mass destruction.[4] Even more plausibly, the Titanic's iceberg spotters must have been convinced that there were no icebergs in sight. And, while there is no justification for their horrific acts, the suicidal 9/11 hijackers may have been truly convinced that their actions would turn them into heroic martyrs in a moral crusade and improve the world order. And, who knows, perhaps Richard Sackler, the so-called King of Oxycontin, sincerely believed he was in the noble business of alleviating pain, rather than causing it on an industrial level. Much in the same way, Elizabeth Holmes, the founder and CEO of Theranos, appeared to genuinely see herself as the Steve Jobs of healthcare.[5]

But self-deception can be used for good as well. Social activists and humanitarian leaders might overestimate the immediate impact of their work, which is crucial for maintaining unwavering commitment. Beleaguered educators might extol their mission of improving the lives of students, even when they're faced with overwhelming obstacles. Philanthropists may even decide to give away billions because of their God complex, while actually being convinced that they are merely altruistic and selflessly interested in improving humanity. The conviction that something is true when it actually isn't also provides innovative and entrepreneurial leaders with a kind of capacity for reality distortion that can inspire and engage others to become followers, along with the abilities to generate prosocial effects and to shape and drive progress.[6]

At the same time, the above examples highlight a fundamental truth: It is not what you think of yourself or your perception of reality that truly matters, nor is it whether you're in touch with your beliefs or act in alignment with them. What ultimately counts is how your actions affect others. Therefore, it makes a lot more sense to judge people not for their thoughts or beliefs, including their accuracy, but for their actions, particularly how they impact others.

The second problem with the "always be honest" mantra is that it's often more advantageous to be dishonest, or at least stretch the truth.[7] Most social exchanges—particularly those that come with meaningful consequences and occur in "high stakes" situations (e.g., first dates, job interviews, critical client presentations, oral examinations in college, or yearly performance reviews)—rarely reward total honesty. In most cases, strategic deception, skilled impression management, conscious self-presentation, and "faking good," will represent a far better alternative, and surer path to success.

Though we hate to admit it, perhaps because we would rather come across as authentic, *in*authentic actions tend to enhance our success and performance, which explains why people are so invested in *not showing* how they really think or feel to others, even as they face external pressure to be transparent.[8] It's much like playing poker: You benefit from bluffing and not showing your hand, while others are eager to decode your hand and determine whether you're bluffing.[9] And, as in poker, it is smart to resist pressures to reveal what others want to know . . .

Back to the negative review from your boss. Between venting, overreacting, and challenging them on this, *or* staying calm, coolheaded, and politely expressing appreciation for their feedback while committing to improving, there is no culture or society where the latter isn't generally preferable. In a similar vein, when organizations put pressure on employees to "be transparent" and provide colleagues with critical negative feedback, engage in difficult conversations, and express their dissent, they inadvertently acknowledge that the prevalent habit and etiquette are exactly the reverse. After all, there would be no need to exert such pressure unless most people had actually learned that it is generally advantageous to pretend, put on a positive front, save face, and be agreeable and nice, even when these reactions aren't spontaneous or authentic. Sure, at times there may well be a need to tell people what they *need* to hear, even when it isn't what they *want* to hear, but the very reason for this need is that people are generally rewarded for not being themselves. That is to say, the pressure to promote transparency is a recognition of its absence—like those customs signs asking us to declare illegal items, "Drug-free zone" signs in the bathroom of a nightclub, or "No peeing" signs at communal swimming pools. If people weren't doing what we don't want them to do, we wouldn't have to remind them. This may be why we idealize authenticity in the first place: We yearn for what we don't have. But there's a logical reason we don't have it, namely that we say we want it, but we don't actually need it or mean it.

Big Little Lies

While society idealizes genuineness, honesty, and transparency, the messy realities of human interaction tend to reward the opposite, even during early childhood. As adults, we pretty much reuse the same deception strategies that we learn as children, despite our parents' persistence in teaching us that honesty is preferable to dishonesty (even when they don't really mean it). Kang Lee, director of the Institute of Child Study at the University of Toronto, classifies children's lies into three main categories:[10]

1. Those that enable us to get along with others, for instance by being kind (e.g., "your baby is cute," "your cake was tasty," and "I love your dog")

2. Those that protect us from potential punishment (e.g., "It wasn't me," "I didn't mean it," and "the dog ate my homework")

3. Self-deceiving lies (e.g., "I am a good person," "it wasn't my fault," and "my dog really loves me")

As adults, we continue to rely on these three types of lies as essential strategies for navigating everyday life. The first two reflect social adjustment and are indispensable in getting along in any society—even though its taboo to admit, and there's a clear social cost to being perceived as a fake. Self-deceiving lies, as we've seen, can be problematic, but they are also essential for deceiving others—delusions, including of grandeur, are often contagious. However, they may eventually create conflicts when others' perceptions of us don't align with our own. Still, competent people will always lie when and as needed, and being aware of their lies may help them remain truthful to themselves, because their deception is focused on others rather than themselves.

For instance, when a job interviewer asks whether you have experience with X or Y, and you make something up, it can reinforce an internal truth: You don't have that experience—which is a weakness—but you can still have confidence in your abilities to compensate for it (e.g., working hard, making an effort to master the task or acquire the skill, etc.) if you get the job, which is more likely if you embellish or inflate your accomplishments during the interview process (so that you will be offered the job). Likewise, if your boss asks if you are busy and you pretend you're swamped, it reminds you that you're not as busy as perhaps you should be. Consider that the main reason for managers' strong preference to abolish working from home is that they take great comfort in watching their employees fake motivation and enthusiasm while they walk past their desks at the office—"My team looks so busy and focused, I'm such a great boss!"[11] As a client of mine noted when she was sent to work from home at the beginning of the Covid-19 pandemic: "But without the office, how will I *pretend* to work?" At the same time, admitting idleness could be misconstrued as poor performance or a lack of motivation, even if the real issue lies with your boss's inability to keep you engaged, or understand how to evaluate what you actually need to produce (output rather than input), both of which suggest that your boss is not sufficiently busy thinking how to motivate you or get the most out of you![12]

Deception would be even more prevalent if lying was easy. As Nietzsche pointed out, lying requires skills, such as a vivid imagination (to craft a compelling story), pretense (to convincingly tell your story), and memory (to keep track of your story), not to mention the ability to suppress authentic emotions like guilt, remorse, and anxiety, especially when you have not lied to yourself.[13] From a skills or ability standpoint, telling the truth is generally easier than lying. As Mark Twain quipped, "If you tell the truth, you don't have to remember anything."[14]

To be effective, inauthentic displays require strong social skills and a willingness to engage in socially desirable behavior. More often than not, people prefer a fake action that is polite, comforting, and prosocial, than a genuine one that violates social norms or etiquettes, or hurts others' feelings or their preferred interpretation of reality. For example, the only possible answer to your friend asking, "Do I look fat in these pants?" is "Are you crazy, of course you don't, you look amazing!" After that, you can gently nudge them toward another ("even better") option, without implying that it has anything to do with their silhouette, or that they looked much better when they were in better shape. In a similar vein, the best way to feel good about our national drug enforcement program is to *not catch* anyone smuggling drugs, so we can maintain the illusion that no drugs are being smuggled. Same goes for children peeing in the pool . . .

Equally, when a friend buys you an underwhelming present for your birthday, but you know she made a real effort to please you after spending a great deal of time and money to get it, you will hopefully have the decency to pretend you love it, and display convincing signs of surprise, gratitude, and happiness—anything else would suggest that you don't care about her, or that you could do with some empathy and social skills coaching.

And when a job interviewer asks you about your biggest weakness, you will hopefully "confess" only to being an incorrigible perfection-ist, possessed workaholic, or way too humble and other-oriented to engage in self-promotion, as opposed to disclosing your real anger management issues, your uncontainable allergy to people who don't think like you, or your profound dislike of stupid interview questions, such as "what are your biggest weaknesses?" After all, you probably don't want to receive a ten out of ten for authenticity or honesty, but a zero out of ten for employability and social skills.

Likewise, the only honest answer to the classic (and not very imag-inative) interview question "Do you enjoy working with others?" is "Well, it obviously depends on who they are," since it is rather un-likely, if not abnormal, for humans to truly enjoy interacting with *every* other human—what is normal and usual, not to mention believ-able, is that we click with some and don't click with others (probably most). However, this type of honesty will likely eliminate you from the candidate shortlist, and rightly so. Why? Because you will be competing against less honest but more socially skilled peers who, in expressing a universal delight and passion for working with abso-lutely anyone and everyone, will come much closer to persuading the interviewer that they are more likely than you to behave in prosocial and team-oriented ways, or at least that they have more polished and refined people skills than you. And they are right: After all, the abil-ity to *pretend* that you love working with others is a fundamental ingredient to effective collaboration and cooperation, especially compared to the *in*ability or unwillingness to pretend just that.[15]

It's pretty simple, really: A job interview, like any other high-stakes social interaction, is not an invitation to express yourself in a genuine or authentic manner. Rather, it's a test of your social, political, and emotional skills, including your willingness to understand and con-form to the informal rules governing interactions with others, and your sensitivity to the interests and feelings of others, as well as existing power dynamics.

This means ignoring the popular self-help advice that you should give your unfiltered or honest opinion to others, except when it comes to trivial and innocuous matters—"Do you prefer chocolate or vanilla ice cream?" or "What did you think of the latest Bridget Jones movie?" (strongly recommend it, by the way) are such exceptions, whereas "What is your take on the current situation in the Middle East?" or "How do you feel about the outcome of the latest political election?" are not.

Crafting and curating an effective interpersonal repertoire—one that results in a positive reputation and enhances your chances of being *regarded* as authentic, as opposed to just feeling good about your self-perceived authenticity—requires emotional labor, the process of managing one's emotions to fulfill the emotional requirements of social interaction, and for the sake of performing your professional role.[16]

Although emotional labor often gets a bad rap when applied to frontline workers like retail staff or restaurant workers—it evokes a sense of capitalist oppression, especially toward the outgroup, low status, or minority candidates (such as the disproportionate demands of "service with a smile" from women rather than men working in hospitality or customer service)—the truth is that we'd all rather deal with people (whoever they are) who excel at their job than those who don't care at all. Fake politeness, especially when you are able to make it come across as real, comes at a considerable psychological or emotional cost—hence the word "labor"—but, just like we appreciate it in others, others appreciate it in us. Moreover, there is an admirable skill in those who are capable of displaying positive artificial emotions toward others at will, as well as suppressing negative ones, without being found out—it is called "emotional intelligence."[17]

Emotional Intelligence > Authenticity

Over the past two decades, thousands of scientific studies have demonstrated that the main quality associated with people—whether it be colleagues, waiters, Uber drivers, bosses, husbands, wives, parents-in-law, or everyone else—who are unwilling or unable to fake it is low emotional intelligence (EQ), a trait that taps into the ability and willingness to modulate our own feelings toward others, and to act in socially desirable, non-impulsive ways.[18]

Though the term was originally popularized as a form of intelligence, there is little scientific support for this idea.[19] In fact, EQ is more like a personality trait, and it measures two basic behavioral tendencies: the tendency to effectively read other people's feelings, and our willingness or capacity to adjust our behavior in response to those feelings. If you are able to understand how others feel, you will be better equipped to adjust your behavior accordingly; and if you are more willing to adjust your behaviors in order to act in a socially desirable way and manage impressions as needed, you will be seen as emotionally intelligent by others.

In line with this theory, a large meta-analysis showed that, empirically speaking, there is practically no difference between being seen as emotionally intelligent, and being effective at impression management.[20] If you give a large group of people a reliable assessment measuring EQ and one measuring impression management, it will be highly unusual for someone to score high on one but low on the other. In other words, if you take a random group of people and rank them on social skills, both assessments (impression management and EQ) will be equally good at predicting where in the ranking or distribution people fall.

As such, evaluating social skills in terms of EQ or impression management is almost as indistinct as measuring the temperature in Celsius or Fahrenheit, or getting the price of something in dollars or euros—the scales, metrics, and denominations may be different, but they are essentially interchangeable and refer to the same thing. Thus, the distinction between EQ and impression management is largely a matter of branding (same wine in different bottles, or even the same bottle but with different labels). Calling it "impression management" has a negative connotation, whereas calling it "EQ" implies a virtue. Still, the point of the matter remains: People who are good at it manage to adjust their behaviors to make a positive impression on others, and are therefore deemed rewarding to deal with.[21] They are not known so much for their honesty as for *appearing* honest, which is a testament to their brilliant impression management skills.

To be sure, if you are so blatantly *in*authentic that everybody can see it, you will not be considered likable or rewarding to deal with at all, because you will come across as a fake, fraud, or phony. However, with a little bit of skill, practice, and deliberation, you may be able to emulate high EQ by carefully curating your public persona in order to tell others what they want to hear, rather than what they need to hear. In other words, there is a very skillful art in telling people what you really think without upsetting them, just like there is a skill to hiding what you really think from them, which requires making your deception *seem* sufficiently genuine, authentic, and honest so that people will buy it.

What matters most is not whether you think you are authentic, but whether *others* think you are—just like what matters in any given situation isn't whether you think you are smart, nice, funny, or competent, but whether *others* think so. "Think" because they will never really know: We may never know whether you are being authentic or not, and neither will you. What we do know, however, is that a higher EQ score will significantly increase the likelihood that you are deemed authentic by others.[22]

This raises an intriguing paradox: Authenticity, often seen as a hallmark of integrity and individuality, can be strategically crafted by actors and exist in the perceptions of an audience. When it is valuable, it exists in the eyes of others rather than as our own personal or subjective experience—it's in the eye of the beholder, or *we*holder, since ideally we should convince more than one person that we are authentic. Moreover, the very tools we use to judge authenticity—emotional intelligence, empathy, and social acumen—are the same tools used to shape others' perceptions, including creating a carefully constructed, but seemingly natural, reputation for being genuine, trustworthy, and . . . authentic. Authenticity, then, is less about who you are and more about how convincingly you project a version of yourself that others find believable and appealing (if not believable, it will be appalling). Whether they are right or not in their opinions of you is not actually relevant, and there is no definitive or clear-cut way of finding that out anyway. Fundamentally, it is simply important for others to feel that they know you, and if you come across as authentic, they will be inclined to think that they do, even if all they consume is your performance. And there's an extra prize if you manage to know or understand how they see you, as it will be key for changing their views on you—assuming that's what you want.

The Curious Case of Phineas Gage

One of the oldest and most famous studies in neuropsychology—the area of behavioral science that deals with the relationship between the brain and behavior—compellingly highlights the tension between social skills on the one hand, and honesty on the other. It's the case of Phineas Gage, a Vermont steel worker who in 1848 suffered a tragic accidental head injury when a steel bar penetrated his skull.[23] Almost miraculously, he managed to not just survive the accident, but recover to the point of nearly regaining his normal capabilities and function in everyday life. But there was one big exception. After the injury, Phineas, who had always been a kind, polite, and gentle person, started to behave in rather rude and obnoxious ways. He lost the ability to self-edit or filter, and would not inhibit any thoughts or feelings when interacting with others.

Despite surviving and being physically fine, Gage became fitful and irreverent, indulged at times in the grossest profanity, manifested little deference for others, was impatient of restraint or advice when it conflicted with his personal desires, and turned obstinate and self-centered. He also showed an unprecedented deficit in his ability to plan and carry out future activities. His decisions became counter-productively impulsive, and he had trouble sticking to his plans. He also demonstrated mood swings and increased aggression and grumpiness. His social relationships were markedly affected. His ability to adhere to social norms and manage personal and professional relationships was significantly compromised.[24] That is to say, Phineas went from being a functional *in*authentic human—which is the norm in every society—to being a dysfunctional authentic anomaly.

While extreme, the Phineas Gage story highlights how much, in order to adapt to any area of life, we depend on our ability to filter our thoughts, control our impulses, and inhibit a great portion of our self. For all the societal pressures to just be ourselves and communicate our honest thoughts and opinions to others, we are lucky to live in a world in which this only happens in small doses.

Embracing Your Inner Meryl Streep and Marlon Brando

Erving Goffman, one of the fathers of modern sociology and a true master at understanding and dissecting social skills, was among the first to emphasize the distinction between lying to ourselves versus lying to others, and how these relate to different approaches to impression management and the presentation of the self in everyday life, even when both are similarly focused on upgrading our reputation with others.[25]

Specifically, Goffman viewed lying to others as "surface acting" (forcing yourself to pretend that you liked the cake when you didn't) and lying to yourself as "deep acting" (persuading yourself that you really liked the cake when you didn't). For a modern example of surface acting, imagine yourself during a Zoom or Teams video conference call, especially when a boring or annoying person—they may even be your boss, an important client, or a potential employer—is speaking. Simply look at yourself on-screen, and notice how much of an effort you are making in displaying fake positive body language signals, trying to convince them and any others on the call that you are highly engaged, following what they are saying in detail, and giving them your undivided attention.

If the above example isn't sufficiently compelling, then try watching a recording of yourself during that conference call, and look at your nonverbal communication signals to note just how unnatural and exaggerated they seem. Irrespective of whether others may deem your expressions authentic or not, they would qualify as surface acting because of your conscious efforts to display them, which, ironically, may actually distract you from what others are saying, and especially what they may be conveying with their own body language, not least if they are surface acting as well!

In contrast, Goffman notes that when we are in deep acting mode, we behave very much like method actors, so immersed in our public persona that our social script becomes our only reality. This technique—perfected by many talented Hollywood actors, such as Meryl Streep, Daniel Day Lewis, and Marlon Brando—involves actors diving deep into their characters, studying them in such detail that they become immersed in them, and often playing their character not just when they are on set filming, but also throughout the extended film production period. They essentially get "under the skin" of the character to effectively become or morph into that character. When deep acting, we are not distracted by any ruminations or second thoughts, as we embody the public role we display for public consumption. In other words, our public self completely takes over our private self or identity, injecting an apparent level of authenticity to our act. Pick your favorite Oscar-winning actor in your favorite movie, and no matter how moved you are by their performance, I suspect you will be able to fathom one thing: It is still a *performance*.

So, just as actors may improve their ability to seem authentic if they are in character all the time and truly immerse themselves in their role, so too is a typical human able to navigate a range of awkward social situations that reward not just sincerity, but also engagement, interest, and admiration, over and above sincerity.

Even the usual list of celebrities embodying the popular archetype of authentic—from Oprah to Obama, Elvis to Madonna, and Beckham to Beyoncé, not to mention Donald Trump and Elon Musk—are more accurately described as great "deep actors," in the sense that their professional persona appears extremely natural, spontaneous, and real. Chances are, though, it is rather different from their personal or private self, or at least one would hope!

If the notion of acting, whether on the surface or in depth, feels morally questionable, or even wrong, it is useful to remember that others are not actually interested in knowing how you feel or think about things "deep down," or who you "really are." Sigmund Freud was interested, though, and he had the genius to make a very good living through his work in psychoanalysis. However, there's a difference between a compelling story about you, me, or people in general, and who we actually are—and since the latter is virtually impossible to know (even Freud failed to convince modern scientists with his theory), it is only the story that matters.

In fact, even when other people tell us that we should behave authentically and say what we really think or feel, they are generally much less interested in who we really are than you may think. Oftentimes, they are even allergic to any facts, truths, or points of view that clash with their preferred ways of interpreting the world. Most people would rather hear you endorse their beliefs and core values than express your beliefs and values if these clash with theirs. And, between honest negative feedback on the one hand, and fake positive feedback that is believable on the other, the latter is usually preferable, not least because honest negative feedback is easy to dismiss as unbelievable! And guess what? You and I are probably just like most people, in that we also prefer to hear good things about ourselves from others, and believe they are true, rather than honest negative or critical things, even when we try very hard to believe they are false . . .

This dynamic completes the self-deception cycle. Not only do we crave positive reinforcement from others, but we also choose to believe it—even when it's delivered with a hint of artifice and a lack of social skills. We reciprocate in return, offering others similarly curated affirmations. This is the unspoken social contract that underpins much of civilized life: We exchange pleasantries and compliments, smoothing over our true feelings to maintain harmony and goodwill. If you dislike this, feel free to go back to the Middle Ages—luckily you can't, but if you could, you would appreciate how far we have come in refining the norms that lubricate social interactions.

Yet, this delicate balance between faking it to please others and coming across as genuine relies on a crucial element: the *believability* of the performance. People are sensitive to insincerity, and detecting a false compliment or disingenuous act can have significant consequences. It damages the perceived trustworthiness of the individual and exposes them as potentially antisocial, thus revealing their "true" feelings as negative or indifferent. The risk is not just losing credibility, but also alienating others who feel betrayed by the façade.

It's a reminder that social interaction is, at its core, a performance—a negotiation between authenticity (in the eyes of others) and artifice (to which others must be oblivious). Mastering this performance is not about maliciously deceiving others, but about recognizing the role we all play in maintaining the social fabric. Deep acting, when done well, can bridge the gap between what is true and what is needed, allowing us to navigate relationships with empathy, tact, and skill. And if you pretend to be someone better than you actually are, then your only concern should be pretending hard enough that you end up becoming that person, overriding the version of you that is no longer on display.

Ultimately, we shouldn't reveal every raw thought or feeling; we should aim to express the version of ourselves that serves the moment and the people around us. It's not about stripping away the performance, but perfecting it to the point where it feels genuine—to others and, perhaps, even to yourself.

But what about radical transparency?

While the Phineas Gage case illustrates the negative impact of deficits in self-control, empathy, and social skills, it is no doubt extreme and, by definition, unrepresentative of well-functioning humans (even if milder versions of Gage may inhabit your workplace). However, there are many modern, non-clinical examples of "extreme authenticity," based on the principle that faking is bad per se, and that there's never much to gain from deception, not least when it forces us to choose short-term consensus at the cost of long-term reality distortion, and leads to a failure to produce creative ideas or innovations. According to this view, a lie may be sweet in the beginning, but bitter in the end, whereas truth is bitter in the beginning, but sweet in the end.

Consider the culture of "radical transparency" popularized by Ray Dalio's Bridgewater hedge fund.[26] In an attempt to eliminate inhibitions to creative and critical thinking, and democratize knowledge sharing and information exchange, Bridgewater—under Dalio's tutelage—urged everybody to express their honest and unfiltered thoughts on any matter, prioritizing radical candor over polite diplomacy.

Conflicts and arguments are simply seen as natural parts of the collective decision-making process, and there is pressure on everyone to state whatever they think, without sugarcoating it and without any regard for politics, etiquette, or hurting people's feelings. It is a sort of "nudist camp" of thoughts and ideas, where employees and managers can act like the post-accident version of Phineas Gage.

Nobody should fake being nice or kind to others for the sheer sake of conforming to their views, aligning with them, or avoiding conflict, because it will reduce logical thinking, introduce noise and bias in decision-making, and lead to groupthink, the state in which people are more interested in fake or sham agreement with others, rather than in reaching the right conclusion or making smart decisions (sort of like in the movie *Death of Stalin*).

The assumption here is that there is no way to leverage the potential power of cognitive diversity and the distributed skills and expertise of the knowledge economy unless people speak freely and candidly about what they think and feel. Therefore, nobody should get offended, defensive, or upset when others state something they dislike, even if these unpleasant or confrontational comments are coming from their own direct reports.

As Dalio himself notes in a popular TED talk, there *are* some limits to how transparent people are (like if a colleague shows you a picture of their newborn baby and you think it's ugly, you probably won't say so). Nonetheless, his radical transparency posits that, overall, truth— or at least people's unfiltered beliefs and opinions about it—ought to trump and eclipse agreeableness, friendliness, and diplomacy, and if you are not thick-skinned enough to tolerate this, you should go work somewhere else.

As a matter of fact, most people do. Not only do they prefer to work in places where radical candor is at best non-existent, and at worst a pretense, they would also prefer to *avoid* spending much time working with people who have no filter, and who relish proving others wrong, even (or especially) if it means belittling them in public.

As the *New York Times* noted, these are cultures of "baroque and dystopic psychological manipulation," which create "a climate of paranoia and punishment that comes down hardest on the weakest."[27] An investigative book and exposé by Rob Copeland revealed that members of the Bridgewater team were asked to rank each other in real time, based on their adherence to Dalio's famed principles, and the team would meet to discuss who was falling short of expectations. This led to a cutthroat environment and high turnover. As Copeland wrote, "[Dalio] was applying his approach to investing rules—testing what worked, and throwing out what didn't—to human resources."[28]

To be sure, the degree to which an employer should be tasked with making people aware of their limitations is an intricate question, not least when we consider the cost of doing so vis-à-vis creating a civil working environment. What is certain is that one is far more likely to achieve this goal if the approach is founded on empathy, kindness, and social skills, which will make people more receptive and open to any form of negative feedback.

Although humans have a tendency to stretch ideas to their extreme—it is a good way to simplify them—most things are better in moderation, and radical transparency is rarely as effective as *moderate* transparency, which is really what we ought to pursue in most livable and tolerable group interactions. That is, just as it is unbearable to interact with someone who is brutally honest all the time, it is also extremely annoying to deal with people who are blatantly faking it all the time, and behaving as if we didn't realize this at all. Extreme truthfulness is as bad as extreme fakeness, just as too much salt is as bad as too little.

As noted, the very fact that we must remind ourselves that it's laudable to be honest with ourselves and others goes to show precisely how easy it is to forget that this *ought* to be the moral ideal we should be pursuing—but attaining it is another thing altogether, requiring delicacy, subtlety, empathy, and practice. So, just as the "Drug-free zone" signs in a nightclub bathroom don't truly aspire to eliminate all drugs from the venue, honesty reminders are mainly attempting to moderate lies and deception and to make them less obvious, rather than completely extinguishing them. The more often we need to repeat the rule, the less likely it is that people are actually following it.

If "truth could set us free," we would have done it already, without any extra persuasion from anyone.[29] We keep banging on about the virtues of honesty because neither we nor others are self-motivated to be honest, but this doesn't mean that we are interested in being blatantly lied to, either. We crave honesty because our workplace lacks it, which is why we cannot seriously assume that when we crave honesty . . . we are making a truthful demand for it! It's a bit like with the "service with a smile" mantra: Most customers prefer it to the reverse, namely honest but grumpy customer service, but they would still prefer to feel that the service with a smile is genuine rather than fake.[30] Same goes for your colleagues: They would prefer to deal with the happy and smiley version of you, than the obnoxious, moody, or irritable one. Yet, at the same time, they may take offense in knowing that the happy and smiley version of you is not genuine.[31]

The point is: You can't have your cake and eat it. And if the choice is between others performing a fairly believable display of niceness and kindness that reflects positively on us, versus a transparent assault on our ego and self-esteem, most of us prefer the former (pessimistic masochists are the exception). So much so, that even when others attempt to provide us with a painful truth, and engage in radical transparency or honest criticism, we will often find ways to distort our interpretation of their feedback so as to digest it without discomfort. No matter how honest others decide to be with us, we can still defend ourselves from reality by simply lying to ourselves, or interpreting reality in an ego-syntonic way.

Research consistently demonstrates a strong workplace preference for agreeableness and kindness. As *The Economist* recently noted: "There is no excuse for unkindness. There is a basic level of decency, civility and courtesy to which everyone is entitled and from which all organizations benefit. Kindness is not a management doctrine. But its absence is a management failure."[32] In line with this finding, large-scale quantitative studies, including meta-analyses of hundreds of independent scientific articles, show that leadership effectiveness and agreeableness—the major personality traits that propel humans to act in polite, kind, diplomatic, and, well, filtered and friendly ways—go hand in hand.[33] Agreeableness has also been linked to ethical behavior, workplace trust, and psychological safety, among other positive outcomes. The reverse also stands: Being direct, unfriendly, transparent, and ignoring how your words impact others—which is the very definition of what being transparent and genuine entails—diminishes trust and integrity perceptions. Likewise, a Stanford University study by Charles O'Reilly and his coauthors reveals a significant correlation between executive agreeableness and organizational performance.[34] Dismantling the "nice guys finish last" myth, they found that agreeable bosses were more likely to lead more collaborative and innovative cultures.

To be sure, there may be some organizational cultures in which nice guys *will* finish last, but few people want to work there. Even in such cultures, being authentic will not necessarily help you climb the ladder, compared to, say, being politically Machiavellian, strategically narcissistic, and selfishly power-focused in an "I'm just in it for myself" sort of way. It's always helpful to strike the right balance. While being nice is preferable to being honest, an excess of niceness can be problematic, not least when it is seen as fake, or it makes others see you as a "pushover." In other words, it's important to *appear* truthful, not just when we are engaging in flattery, ingratiation, and praise, but also when we are showcasing our competitive drive and motivation to achieve.[35]

Trust is more important than authenticity

Trust is the essence of social exchange, and the fundamental lubricant of interpersonal relations.[36] If we don't trust others, we cannot collaborate. And without collaboration, there is no progress or functioning society. While it's common to assume that trust requires us to understand or know what people feel or think "deep down," this isn't the case. Trust is warranted simply by being able to predict how other people will act or behave in high-stake situations, especially toward us.

In the real world, there are plenty of examples illustrating how our trust in other people is a prerequisite for depending on them.

For instance, when taking a flight, I don't need the airline to provide me with proof that the pilots on duty genuinely like Argentine psychologists, or have no personal animosity against Latin American men in their 40s. In fact, I am perfectly relaxed getting on any plane, even if the pilots actually dislike people who, like me, belong to those groups.

By the same token, when I open my mouth to let my dentist perform a root canal on me, I do it without much consideration of whether she is truly interested in making me feel better, or simply performing her job—and, given the pain she inflicts on me, I would take little consolation from knowing that she's doing it out of her heartfelt and passionate interest in my health and well-being, or that she really loves my sense of humor.

Likewise, when I give money to a homeless person, I assume that they don't care so much whether I do it out of guilt, compassion, or a need to feel good about myself, or simply because I find it annoying to carry loose change in my pocket. In essence, we can get by perfectly fine in most everyday-life situations without discovering or knowing other people's ulterior motives, because this simply isn't necessary to trust others.

Trust happens not through some magical psychic power that enables us to know how other people feel or think deep down, but through our ability to pick up consistent patterns in how others behave, which is only enabled by their tendency to behave in consistent ways. As Aristotle famously noted, "We are what we repeatedly do."

Conversely, trust breaks when our expectation of how people ought to behave is broken, either by their willingness to break their usual behavioral pattern (meaning, they acted in unpredictable ways), or by our assumptions or working model of them being wrong or mistaken (meaning, we made invalid inferences). For example, punctual people (I am proud to be one of them) are usually annoyed at people who are always late. But, so long as they are *always* late, you can always plan around it, so there's no reason to be annoyed (except with yourself if you fail to plan around it). The problem arises when you have to plan for their predicted arrival time, but they break their pattern. Take, for example, someone who is always late, but decides to arrive punctually the one time that you got there late (precisely to avoid waiting) and inevitably, they will complain that you were late then, that one time! Equally, you can always take the necessary precautions when you are driving behind someone who clearly looks like a reckless or incompetent driver. The problem arises when someone who seems like a cautious, competent, and reliable driver suddenly performs a reckless maneuver. As the Norwegians say: "There's no such thing as bad weather, only the wrong choice of clothing." Along the same lines, whatever others do is less problematic when you can predict it. The famous adage, "Fool me once, shame on you; fool me twice, shame on me," captures the issue well.

The mind works in mysterious ways. We can barely make sense of our own, let alone the minds of others, and yet, we continuously operate as if we can. Although our desire may be to infer intention in others, our best bet is to assume that they intended to act the way they did, while remaining agnostic about their ulterior motives. After all, who cares about the *why* if you can get the *what* and *how* right most of the time? A bit of humility would be good here: We are not aspiring to be Freud, but simply people who have a practical interest in getting along with others, which can happen if we understand them on some basic level—getting a sense of what they do in different situations is more than enough.

In fact, once we go beyond the level of observable behavior, we are bound to encounter a multiplicity of meanings, including a complex web of potential motivations and motives, which would take too long to scrutinize and dissect. So, if a colleague is always nice to us at the office cafeteria, it may be tempting to think that they like us. However, there could be many other reasons for their niceness, including some that don't require their emotions to be genuine. For example, they may want a favor from us; they may be intimidated by us; they may mistake us for someone else, or make false attributions about our persona; they may think that we like them; and so on. What we may assume, though, is that they are acting in their best interest, in the sense that, for whatever reason, they prefer to be nice to us than not— the *why* is beyond our grasp. We may also assume that it's in their best interest to seem genuine, whatever their ulterior motives may be.

The reason for this is straightforward: If they were unable to come across as real or genuine, we would have good reason to distrust them, and also distrust our own predictions of their behavior. After all, the notion that they are not genuine implies that they are forcing themselves to behave in a way they may not want, which makes our expectations more vulnerable, and our predictions more fragile and unreliable.

In short, we are under societal pressures to be nice and genuine, but oftentimes we will experience a tension between the two, leaving us with the option of either not being nice, or faking genuineness. However, if we are found out, we will pay a high reputational tax, namely becoming less trustworthy to others. Indeed, one of the main deterrents of lying is the fear of being found out, since even a one-off incident can permanently destroy one's credibility and reputation. The risk of being caught while lying is evident, and it clearly comes at a high price, namely a strong devaluation of one's assumed character and others' trust in you.

Contrary to what we may think, it is not honesty or truth, but the ability to trust people that we really care about. And, when it comes to trust, truth is not a prerequisite; in fact, it may actually be a hindrance. We are so accustomed to sustaining semi-truths or socially acceptable departures from facts and reality, mostly in the name of prosocial behaviors or acts of politeness, that if we suddenly started to be honest with others, they would change their opinion of us.

The Choice Is Yours

Even if effort is required to modulate your behavior and act in a way that doesn't just communicate your thoughts and ideas, but also does so in a way that is palatable to others and showcases your emotional, political, and social skills, it is well-worth it.

Don't fall into the trap of thinking that you are special enough to disregard how you impact others, or that others want to see the unfiltered version of you. Sure, there is a big market for tabloid photos of celebrities looking disheveled and terrible when caught by paparazzi—but they are rich and famous celebrities, and we are not (if you are, I take that back).

The schadenfreude we feel when we see these images is based on the fact that celebrities usually look so great, so it's cathartic to remind ourselves that they are still like us, imperfect creatures who must make a big effort to present themselves in the best possible way . . . all while making it seem natural. In this way, you can think of social skills and EQ as a kind of Instagram filter for your character or personality: The real you is still there, on display, but in the most desirable and user-friendly way. And unlike actual Instagram, this filter is an integral part of your personality. Amy Cuddy, a popular thought-leader and self-help author, tells us that "authenticity doesn't just mean you're not filtering what you're saying, it's about being able to know and access the best parts of yourself and bring them forward."[37] Although her nuance introduces an important reconfiguration of the colloquial meaning of authenticity, it is certainly a better recipe for success, both at the personal and collective level, than the "always be honest" trap.

3

Trap 2

Be True to Your Values and Follow Your Heart No Matter What

We may have innate "yuck" reactions that helped our ancestors survive, at a time when they were social mammals but not yet human. Those reactions will not always be a reliable guide to right and wrong in the much larger and more complex global community in which we live today. For that, we need to use our ability to reason.

—Peter Singer, *Ethics in the Real World*

Humans naturally gravitate toward their own values—core principles that shape how we view the world and determine what we consider right or wrong. These values act as a lens through which we interpret and evaluate our own experiences and those of others, a sort of inner moral compass through which we interpret whether something is good or bad, including our own actions.

Intuitively, most people would agree that staying true to one's values, and expressing them through words and actions, is not just right, but also admirable. So, when asked whether it's preferable for someone to be true to their values, and express these honest feelings through their opinions, behaviors, and habits, the average person would not hesitate to agree; to the point that the reverse, someone who just fails to follow their heart or core beliefs, almost certainly indicates moral corruption.

Indeed, when we think of someone as being in a situation in which they don't follow their values—such that they violate their own principles or act in accordance with external forces that align with an incompatible, or at least different, range of values—it is tempting to quickly dismiss this person as a fraud, phony, or impostor. For instance, if you see a work colleague being treated unfairly by your boss, it would be more honorable to speak up and confront your boss than to just be a bystander. Likewise, if a client praised you for a job that was actually done by a colleague of yours, and you felt that this credit was undeserved, it would be more honorable to give credit to your colleague than to accept the undeserved praises. Moreover, if your boss assessed your performance as "exceptional," when in fact you didn't think of it so highly, it would be more noble of you to state that you don't deserve such strong praise than to accept your boss's views (and reject the related bonus).

The "follow your heart and be true to your values" mantra implies that so long as our decisions and behaviors are a sincere expression of our core beliefs, they are not just authentic, but also good, if not moral, ethical, and noble. But the idea that we must always stay true to our values and act in line with our beliefs—known in philosophy as "moral authenticity"—runs the risk of placing one's personal ethics above societal moral standards. In some instances, we may see the benefit and logic to this: for example, when conforming to a majority means being an amoral or immoral bystander who perpetuates dominant injustices; or when your values protect you from mimicking questionable or toxic behaviors—as entrepreneur and coach Patty

Azzarello recently noted to me, "Even when I worked in really bad cultures, I lived by my 'don't be an a--hole' rule." However, there are many other instances, particularly in the corporate world, where the reverse may be true—namely, using the "live by your values" rule as an excuse to get away with selfish and antisocial behavior, and in effect preferring one's own spoiled and entitled motives over the prosocial communal rule. No client has ever said this to me, but I suspect quite a few people may live by the "don't give a sh-t about others" rule, or a least that seems to be the value or principle that would explain their behaviors. A milder version of this postmodern ideal is also reflected in phrases like "It's my truth" or "That's not how *I* see it," which prioritize individual perspectives over objective facts and reality, not to mention the interests or perspectives of others.

Values Gone Wrong

While imposing our own selfish values on others or using them to dismiss other people's values is usually a sign of immaturity, the consequences of doing so are particularly severe when one's values and beliefs are antisocial and parasitic to begin with, and is further exacerbated when such people occupy positions of status or power. As history repeatedly shows us, powerful people become particularly destructive when they decide to be true to their toxic values, especially when they manage to convince themselves—not to mention others—of the legitimacy of their actions, allowing them to dress up or present their narcissistic delusions as noble pursuits.

For example, CEOs may pay themselves a fortune, but keep employees' salaries extremely low, under the pretext of being customer-centric, beating competitors with lower prices, and making money for their shareholders, which in their view would justify the exorbitant

compensation. Andrew Carnegie, the Scottish-American industrialist, justified his decision to pay workers poorly by saying it would leave
him with more money to build museums, libraries, and universities—
otherwise, he reasoned, his workers would just spend the extra money
on booze. Likewise, a billionaire may refuse to pay taxes because "the
system is rigged," "the state is corrupt," or tax avoidance is legal (not
to mention the fact that other rich people do this as well), thus leading them to ask, "Why should I be the only fool to pay them?" And
the bosses of a company that manufactures harmful products—
that they managed to get approval for through political lobbying and
donations—may convince themselves and others that there's nothing
wrong with this, since it's technically not illegal.

Examples abound among political leaders as well, such as the case
of the democratically elected populist politician who uses their power
and support to put in place economic or social policies, or engage in
international conflict or wars, that end up harming their own people,
but solidifies their power, status, and influence, and advances their
own personal interests, in the process.[1] While one doesn't know if such
political figures can sleep peacefully at night, it is highly probable that
they do, precisely because they are acting in line with their values.

Alas, these and too many other nefarious examples underscore the
many ways in which unchecked power combined with moral ratio-
nalization can lead to systemic exploitation, inequality, and harm, all
while cloaked in a veneer of legitimacy or public benefit.

Outspoken Leaders

Authenticity, in the sense of being true to one's values, is also important at the organizational or corporate level, with a great deal of recent research examining whether businesses "put their money where

their mouth is" when it comes to Environmental, Social, and Governance (ESG), Corporate Social Responsibility (CSR), or any other brand-boosting exercise meant to persuade consumers and investors that they are not just in business in order to make money, but also—if not primarily—trying to make the world a better place.[2]

Research shows that employees are more likely to believe in their employers' prosocial aspirations and claims, when these actually align with their employers' internal culture.[3] For instance, a company that champions diversity and inclusion in its marketing campaigns, but lacks any diversity among its leaders (sadly, more common than it should be), will not be seen as authentic by its employees. As it turns out, many of those companies have recently decided to make a sudden switch or shift from being passionate advocates of diversity and inclusion (perhaps their previous attempt at impression management?), to categorically ditching their programs altogether (perhaps their authentic belief?), thus suggesting that there were rational reasons for skepticism among employees and the wider public. As is generally the case, the problem is not when you fake it, but rather when you stop, because your authentic beliefs will be found out, which may come at a considerable cost—the confirmation that you weren't authentic or honest in the first place. Likewise, an organization that seems committed to wellness and well-being, but has no qualms overworking its employees to the point of burnout or emotional breakdown, will rightly be seen as disingenuous or inauthentic by its workforce, including those who are lucky to not burn out. Same goes for the many organizations that radically and suddenly changed, if not mostly eliminated, their work-from-home policies. In general, when brands are perceived as "virtue signaling"—making gratuitous or empty identity claims not backed by appropriate actions or substance—their efforts will backfire and raise consumer distrust.[4]

In fact, it is not even sufficient for a brand to engage in prosocial or altruistic behaviors—consumers must *perceive* their efforts as actually genuine.[5] Importantly, amid much pressure on leaders to "speak up" on sensitive and controversial issues (e.g., Israel and Palestine, abortion, gender diversity, Donald Trump, Elon Musk, and even work-from-home policies), and to "express their true values"—as if these were a natural proxy for the values of the organization or cultural DNA of their companies—it is helpful to consider the nontrivial possibility that employees, as well as clients and consumers, may not always align with the values of the company and its leader.

For instance, Bob Iger's decision to step down from President Trump's advisory council in 2017, following Trump's announcement that the United States would withdraw from the Paris Climate Accord, was a political statement that had mixed reactions. Same goes for the recent decision of Mark Zuckerberg to ditch Meta Platforms' corporate approach to improving diversity and inclusion, in alignment with the values of the second Trump presidency (the first also, actually). Whatever leaders decide to do and communicate, and whatever the reasons they give for such decisions, it is clear that some consumers, voters, and citizens will praise their moves, while others will complain or feel antagonized.

Some Other Examples . . .

In 2018, following the Parkland school shooting, Dick's Sporting Goods CEO Ed Stack announced that they would stop selling assault-style rifles and high-capacity magazines, and would no longer sell any guns to people under 21. This decision was met with both acclaim and significant backlash, especially from pro-gun consumers who felt betrayed by the company.

Same goes for Starbucks CEO Howard Schultz launching a 2015 antiracism campaign where baristas were encouraged to write "Race

Together" on coffee cups in order to spark conversations about race with customers. The campaign faced widespread criticism as many felt it was inappropriate and overly simplistic for a coffee shop setting, leading to a considerable consumer backlash.

The craze about expressing personal and corporate values and being true to one's core beliefs has put CEOs in a very difficult position—doomed if they speak, and doomed if they don't, unless they manage to find a way to elegantly sit on the fence. Faced with polemical issues, no matter what CEOs do, they will alienate certain members of the public, all for the sake of cementing a cult-like relationship with the employees or consumers who expect them to act like tribal crusaders or moral ambassadors of their cause.

Fundamentally, the notion that CEOs, and leaders more broadly, need to tell us how they feel deep down about issues that are not related to work, their company's business, or their employees' jobs, seems hard to justify, unless we accept that we are putting those corporate leaders in the role of a parent or a religious/moral/cult leader, and that the typical level of maturity among employees, subordinates, and followers is rather low. After all, only in an infantilized world would we need corporate executives to tell us how we ought to feel or think about societal matters, or expect them to act as spokespeople for our own values and beliefs.

When you are a CEO, by putting your money where your mouth is when it comes to expressing your core beliefs or values, it is a sure recipe to alienate people who think or feel different on those matters, and it harms genuine efforts to create a diverse and inclusive culture (more on this in chapter 8). Rather than proudly shouting how they feel or think about wider moral issues that barely concern their organization's work, such leaders would be better off expressing their respect and tolerance for people who feel differently about moral matters, which is better achieved by not saying anything rather than picking sides. Indeed, there is a big difference between allowing thinking and thinking aloud—the more leaders engage in the latter, the less they incentivize followers to engage in the former.

In that sense, we may arrive at a pretty contrarian conclusion about moral authenticity, diametrically opposed to the notion that acting on the basis of one's moral convictions is ethical. As a matter of fact, having the ability to question your own moral values, and to refrain from strong convictions in order to examine, understand, and respect people with different values—which by definition involves scrutinizing your own values and beliefs, and understanding their potential relative or subjective nature—is surely more desirable, not just for your own sake, but for the sake of any tolerant society in which people from different backgrounds and beliefs learn to *coexist* in harmony.

Respecting *Other* People's Values

If we are truly serious about the "always be true to your values" rule, we should examine what would happen when we apply it to *other* people's values, particularly those who don't share our values.

For starters, when we start with an understanding or realization that not everybody shares the same values—which is the very point of this tenet, namely to act according to *your* values rather than others'—then the inherent assumption here is that we must not make compromises of any sorts, that we ought to resist pressure to conform to other people's beliefs, and that we need to, above all, remain faithful to our own beliefs, unless we are happy to live our lives like a fraud.

However, this rule should not just apply to us, but also to others, which would basically result in a society in which, without exception, nobody adjusts their behaviors to other people's values, and everybody ends up associating only with people who share their own values and beliefs—because it would be impossible to connect or relate to people who not only think differently than us, but are also intolerant of those who think differently than them.

Instead of being true to your values, how about being open to questioning them?

Being true to your values would also entail only picking romantic partners, including spouses, who are like us in terms of class, political orientation, and race—a sure recipe for making the world more closed-minded and intolerant.[6] Any society with aspirations to accept and assimilate people from different walks of life and with different beliefs systems—including different religions, cultures, nationality, and even individual ethical codes—can only exist if people learn to accept, or at least tolerate, other people's values.

This means making compromises, which involves censoring our own wishes, preferences and behaviors, questioning our own beliefs, particularly when they are more like convictions, and suspending our own preferences or choices in order to make concessions to accommodate others. It also means not imposing our values on others, and being able to bend our behaviors for the sake of attaining harmony with other people's values and beliefs.

The ability to act according to other people's values also brings huge benefits to organizations and workplaces, as groups that are composed of individuals with divergent or diverse values have more potential to function effectively, especially in unpredictable, challenging, and complex environments. Setting aside social, economic, and moral reasons for encouraging a more diverse workplace, there is no better incentive for promoting diversity than the premise that diverse teams and organizations are more creative. When two people think alike, one of them is unnecessary.

Diverse teams have an advantage when it comes to creativity and innovation, because people from different backgrounds, origins, and walks of life are more likely to add value to their teams by providing original, otherwise neglected, points of view and ideas.[7] Although it is always easier to manage people when they are similar, since one size will fit all, the secret ingredient to creating something novel and harnessing innovation, which provides the seeds to progress and the evolution of any organization and society, is to mix things that don't usually or naturally go together, or haven't been combined in the past—and these "things" include humans. One of the advantages the United States has historically enjoyed over Europe (now also China) when it comes to innovation, especially over the past century, is that it is far more heterogeneous and diverse, not just demographically, but as a society, culture, and system as well. If you don't allow for random variation, you will not get any exciting innovation—but you have to also allow for the possibility that random variation fails or results in no innovation at all, which is far more likely in the United States than in Europe.

With people becoming more polarized, antagonistic, tribal, and intellectually self-radicalized—things we can usually observe very well in others, but not as much in ourselves—we would certainly do well to consider the advantages of moderating our adherence to our own values. Although, I should note, the tendency to regard other people as moral or intellectual extremists probably says more about our own tendency to be in that same category (but at the other extreme) than it does about being moderate.

Voltaire aptly noted that "doubt is not a pleasant condition, but certainty is absurd."[8] Were he alive today, he would probably be surprised by the rarity of doubt in our times, particularly in relation to the prevalence of certainty, not least because certainty is more than ever disconnected from facts or reality—despite the fact that we have never had as much access to data, information, and records of reality as we do today.

Paradoxically, in an age of ubiquitous information, it is easier than ever to be uninformed or misinformed. And while scientific knowledge is advanced incrementally by highlighting nuances and discovering the hidden forces that make complex phenomena intelligible, we have become less tolerant of ambiguity and cling to categorical interpretations of the world, which suppress any doubts. "Never in doubt, yet always wrong" is a far more common affliction today than any of its alternatives, and people are rarely shy about expressing their moral values, even in the absence of knowledge about a given topic.

Confidence trumps competence, and the capacity for self-doubt and self-criticism is oddly seen as a sign of weakness. The notion that someone can be an effective leader when they admit that they don't know the answer to any questions seems ludicrous to the general public. Conversely, we appear to have no problem electing leaders who, even if it's not true, tell us that everything is under control and that they understand what to do, so long as those leaders seem aligned with our values.

For the most part, our ability to coexist with others who think differently from us was largely enabled by social etiquette, cultural norms, and tolerance. Whatever happened to smiling and being nice to your neighbor when you see them, but moaning about them in the privacy of your home? The same applies to work colleagues and bosses: If you disagree with them on social policy, religion, ideology, political and moral issues, not to mention sports and movies, who cares? It should still be possible for you to get along with them in a professional environment, and put aside your ideological differences in order to collaborate effectively.

To some degree, you can exchange opinions and move on, but if that is too much to ask, or they seem intolerant or allergic to your views, you can simply *pretend* to go along, in the most convincing way you can. Rest assured you will find plenty of people you can complain to and who will provide cathartic ears for your whining, because they either think like you, or are capable of reassuringly pretending they do, a skill that aligns with the anti-authenticity approach described in chapter 2.

To be sure, navigating the delicate line between our own moral convictions, and tolerating others, has occupied every moral philosopher in history. Karl Popper wrote extensively about the matter, with lucid rationality and compelling moral substance, as shown here:

> Unlimited tolerance must lead to the disappearance of tolerance. If we extend unlimited tolerance even to those who are intolerant, if we are not prepared to defend a tolerant society against the onslaught of the intolerant, then the tolerant will be destroyed, and tolerance with them.
>
> We should therefore claim, in the name of tolerance, the right not to tolerate the intolerant. We should claim that any movement preaching intolerance places itself outside the law, and we should consider incitement to intolerance and persecution as criminal, in the same way as we should consider incitement to murder, or to kidnapping, or to the revival of the slave trade, as criminal.[9]

Thus, instead of being true to your values, how about being open to other people's values, or at least tolerating them? The world is already full of ideological, dogmatic, and fanatical people who are so stubbornly and possessively attached to their values that they repel anyone who thinks or feels different from them, opting instead for further intellectual isolation and radicalization—which modern technologies facilitate—in digital echo chambers and AI-sheltered cocoons, where all they can see and hear is their values on steroids, amplified to the extreme.

You're probably not being logical

Jonathan Haidt, a prominent social psychologist at NYU, explores the concept of moral reasoning in his book, *The Righteous Mind: Why Good People Are Divided by Politics and Religion*. His central thesis revolves around the idea that moral judgments stem more from intuitions and emotions than from logical reasoning.

Haidt suggests that people are primarily driven by instinctive moral intuitions, and they use post hoc reasoning to justify these intuitions. To illustrate the relationship between intuition and reasoning, Haidt uses the metaphor, borrowed from the Scottish philosopher David Hume, of a rider (representing conscious reasoning) on an elephant (representing intuition). The rider can guide the elephant, but is ultimately led by the elephant's immediate reactions and directions. This metaphor encapsulates how rational thought often serves to justify and rationalize our gut feelings and visceral judgments, rather than guide them.[10] In this way, Haidt argues that moral reasoning is largely emotional and irrational, "intuitions come first, strategic reasoning second." This concept is rooted in the psychological principle that emotional responses occur quicker than rational thought, suggesting that most moral decisions are based on immediate intuitions, rather than deliberate reasoning.

Central to Haidt's argument is the Moral Foundations Theory, which he developed with colleagues.[11] This theory suggests that there are several innate psychological systems—or moral foundations—that underlie moral judgments. These foundations are Care/Harm, Fairness/Cheating, Loyalty/Betrayal, Authority/Subversion, and Sanctity/Degradation. Haidt argues that different cultures and political groups emphasize these foundations differently, which helps explain variation in moral values and polarization in politics and religion.

Moral systems are largely shaped by the need to foster cohesive and cooperative groups. This groupism influences our moral intuitions, often leading to a kind of "hive mind" that prioritizes group norms and values. Haidt's work also delves into the understanding of moral diversity. His model emphasizes that recognizing the different moral foundations can lead to greater empathy and understanding between individuals and groups with conflicting moral perspectives. By understanding that others might be operating from different moral foundations, it becomes easier to appreciate their viewpoints and find common ground. However, this requires a minimum baseline of empathy, whereby people are not inclined to ignore others and what they think, but actually make an effort to understand them, including their thoughts and feelings.

Let me clear my throat

The idea of staying true to one's values and following one's heart resonates deeply in modern culture, and is often celebrated as a hallmark of authenticity and integrity. However, in an interconnected and diverse world, moral authenticity must be balanced with humility, self-reflection, and a willingness to question one's values. Tolerance and an openness to understanding the perspectives of others are not signs of moral compromise, but rather essential components of fostering inclusive and harmonious societies, teams, and organizations.

We need to adopt a more nuanced approach: one that prioritizes critical self-examination, empathy for others, and the flexibility to adapt to differences. By embracing these principles, individuals and leaders alike can move beyond self-serving rationalizations and contribute to a world where diversity of thought and mutual respect thrive.

4

Trap 3

Don't Worry About
What Others Think of You

Always this subtle criticism and appraisal of other people,
this analysis of other people's motives.

—D. H. Lawrence

We're often told to stop caring about what others think of us, especially if their views are critical of us or differ from our self-perception.
Adapting to others' needs, beliefs, or expectations is framed not just
as inauthentic, but as a betrayal of our true selves, which is perceived
as cowardice and morally flimsy.

This perspective—captured in the third authenticity trap along
the lines of "stop worrying about what people think of you"—
celebrates bold tales of creative disruptors, rebel talent, and moral
crusaders who opposed tyrannic regimes or the status quo, and thus
created a better state of affairs and brought much-wanted progress to
the masses. Its adherents will point to the inspirational influence of

eminent innovators, moral leaders, and disruptive game changers in fields as wide-ranging as science, politics, arts, business, and sports.

And yet, rebellious instincts and creative achievements are not as directly and strongly related as we like to think. To be sure, without a great deal of talent or an even greater dose of dedication and effort—both of which are critical to harnessing talent in the first place—your rebellious nonconformism and tendency to defy the status quo will be a liability, rather than an asset. This is why Nick Kyrgios is nowhere near as accomplished as Serena Williams, but instead a failed promise and wasted talent. While both seem authentic in the sense of "sticking it to the status quo" and using their brand and charisma to defy norms, Serena excelled and broke all tennis records thanks to her dedication to being a serious professional, much more focused on perfecting her game and developing a winning mindset, which included the ability to (mostly) manage her passionate outbursts and anger. Kyrgios, on the other hand, simply refuses to grow up. He is so good at disregarding what people think of him, that he chooses to party rather than train, and live a hedonistic and fun life unconstrained by the demands of professional tennis. Good for his happiness? Perhaps, but a disappointing curse for his professional career.

If we shift to the arts, specifically to Frida Kahlo, it is true that "fitting in" would have meant sacrificing much of what made her work and life so distinctive. It would have required her to suppress her individuality, her political beliefs, and her deep personal expression, which were central to her identity as an artist. Instead of becoming a trailblazing figure, she might have become just another artist following the trends of the time, with her unique voice and perspective lost in the process.

That said, most jobs and occupations have little in common with the arts, except that career advancement is not just determined by talent, but by networking, joining influential groups, and being mentored or sponsored by those who are part of the status quo, even if they represent a different part of the status quo than the one you are trying to bring down. In Kahlo's case, she received such sponsorship from her husband Diego Rivera, who was already an acclaimed and famous artist, beloved by Mexico's jet set. He became one of her key sponsors, introducing her to the international circle of eminent artists and collectors, and playing a key role in shaping her brand and career. Without his influence, Frida's remarkable talents may have flown under the radar, as was the case with Vincent Van Gogh, Modigliani, and Vermeer, all of whom produced some of the world's most expensive works of art, but, being purely focused on their art, they were perhaps not bothered enough to network, win the establishment over, or "socialize" their talents, so they lived in precarious financial conditions.

Additionally, while Steve Jobs may be the business icon for rebellious non-conformity, there is far more nuance to his style and leadership than meets the eye. For starters, Jobs was one of the most customer-obsessed entrepreneurs in modern times, defying conventional design and mainstream technology with the aim to deliver a superior experience to consumers. In the process, he turned Apple into the world's most valuable brand. Perhaps he simply allowed himself to ignore colleagues when they disagreed, and to be rude to competitors and investors, but he did so through caring more about what people thought of his products (and him) than they actually did.

We must also remember that Steve Jobs differed from other businesspeople, leaders, and entrepreneurs, not only in his arrogance and questionable interpersonal skills and style, but in his brilliant vision and talent as well. As you probably won't be surprised to hear, there is no shortage of people in the world with the same level of ego, self-centered volatility, and obnoxious and rude management style held by Jobs, but they typically aren't geniuses like him (if you wish, add

Elon Musk to this small and unrepresentative bucket). In fact, the thing these untalented peers may share with Jobs is that their grumpy and entitled tantrums also make them quite unemployable—they may be destined for self-employment, but are unlikely to create the next Apple. It should be noted that Jobs, like many entrepreneurs, had to create his own company because his problems with authority made it hard for him to follow rules and take directions from others, and he even managed to be fired from his own company twice. If this sounds romantic and heroic, that is purely because, in the case of Jobs, the story has a rare happy ending.

But in most instances, a temperament as such will just lead to failure and dispositional unemployability. Incidentally, when Tim Cook, who has a much softer, gentler, and more prosocial style than Steve Jobs, took over as CEO of Apple, popular belief was that it may signal the end of Apple—how else could a firm manage to remain successful when it was forced to switch from that iconic visionary rock star of innovation to a rather boring, accountant-looking corporate business leader? Turns out Apple has become much more successful and valuable under Cook ($3.35 trillion today) than Jobs ($350 billion when he died in 2011), which should not surprise anyone. Of course, we will never know how successful Apple would be today if it were still run by Steve Jobs, but it should not surprise anyone that Tim Cook's leadership accelerated, rather than slowed down, his success. After all, qualities such as empathy, kindness, emotional intelligence, and the ability to manage yourself and others, are key enablers of leadership effectiveness, and might explain Tim Cook's brilliant success.

Note that even Jobs became a much better leader—and more successful businessperson—during his final years, when he showed an unprecedented ability to tame his demons and dark side, and displayed clear signs of maturity and stability, as opposed to always being at war with competitors and trying to be the center of the world.

There is rarely much to learn from exceptional case studies or outliers, especially compared to large-scale scientific studies that focus on people who are much closer to the average person and typical leader or entrepreneur. This also includes occupations that are very different from being a rock star, famous artist, elite athlete, or billionaire entrepreneur. It is much more about normal professions, work experiences, and careers, where your rebellious instincts and non-conformist attitudes will only be tolerated within reason, provided you have the talent to back it up, and the social skills to smooth them out so they are expressed as interesting or positive features of your personality—assuming people still feel they can trust you, and that you will not put your own selfish interests ahead of their own needs.

Whether you work in an office or are lucky enough to enjoy the freedom to work from home or anywhere else, your colleagues and clients will appreciate a certain etiquette when it comes to dress code (e.g., you can ditch the tie or be slightly more informal than most, but not show up in your underwear or beach attire), communication style (e.g., they will prefer if you don't speak over them and listen, and that you show some interest and attention in what they say), and rule-abiding (indeed, just as Serena Williams had to adhere to the rules of tennis, you will benefit from doing what your boss asks you to do, even if you think the world would be a better place if you didn't).

Blame It on Sartre

The philosophical foundation of "don't worry about what others think of you" can be traced back to Jean-Paul Sartre, who equated authenticity to radical freedom. Sartre was a romantic, albeit of the French existential variant. In today's times, we would probably find him wearing a Che Guevara t-shirt, smoking weed, and sipping his almond milk cortado in a hipster coffee joint in Williamsburg, Hackney, or Le Marais, while talking compellingly about the demise of capitalism. Or perhaps, since this archetype has now become more of a social norm than a cultural oddity, would he be more like Jordan Peterson (a contrarian provocateur who is as grumpy as he is moralistic, but enjoys rock star status among millions of followers who fail to truly understand him 75 percent of the time)? Jokes aside, we have become accustomed to Sartre's notion that neglecting societal rules and norms is associated with higher moral status and a kind of character attractiveness that stands in diametric opposition to the mindless sheep-like conformist who lacks personality, not to mention "cojones."

If we are so obsessed with what others think of us that we end up acting like an inhibited, repressed, and self-restrained bore, then life won't be much fun, and we may risk coming across as losers, empty suits, or fake politicians. However, there is a wide gap in the spectrum between this state of being and Sartre's notion of radical freedom. Besides the archetypal and clichéd examples of cultural heroes embodying a rock star approach to life (such as Jim Morrison, Amy Winehouse, Naomi Campbell, Kurt Cobain, and Anthony Bourdain), there aren't many true examples of people who were oblivious to others' impressions or judgments of them.

In fact, what Sartre and all of the above examples have in common serves as proof that there's often a very thin line between conforming and being a non-conformist. The only way to rebel against something is to be aware of it, as that is your only option for resisting its influence, and resisting having an influence over it (if you hope to change it). As Slavoj Zizek noted, "We are what we negate," in the sense that our enemies, dislikes, and nemeses—whether real or imagined—define us as much as our loves and convictions. Incidentally, there is a beautiful irony in the fact that when we tell people to ignore what others think or say, we are still telling them what to do . . .

In any case, there's being *unhappy* with the rules, and actually *wanting* to change them—and there's wanting, versus trying, not to mention actually succeeding. Note that each of these scenarios requires one to understand the rules, which is impossible if you decide to ignore them. And actually changing the rules will usually require one to work within them—that is, one has to master the rules of the game before one can change them. As Pablo Picasso famously noted, "Learn the rules like a pro, so you can break them like an artist." On the invention of cubism, he added: "It took me four years to paint like Raphael, but a lifetime to paint like a child."

One of the oldest findings in behavioral science is that behavior is always a function of both the person (including their character traits, values, etc.) and the situation they are in (the environments in which our behavior takes place, such as a church, nightclub, home, or office).[1] Although there's an infinite number of situations, since each situation is unique, for the most part, situations always concern other people. And even if you decide to ignore these other people and instead act purely according to your own independent impulses, needs, and wishes, this will not stop them from paying attention to what you do, and indeed figuring out who you are, what you are like, and whether it is beneficial for them to interact with you. You may not like people judging you, but that won't stop them from doing so. If you want to change their judgments, it is useful to understand where they are coming from.

Eccentricity is sometimes accepted, tolerated, and even celebrated, but it is more often censored and condemned. In fact, the very reason we celebrate and promote eccentricity at times is that it is fairly uncommon, similar to how rule-breaking of any kind is applauded in inverse proportion to its occurrence. For instance, the cultural acceptance of rule-breaking differs from one society to another, but it is never beneficial to make rule-breaking the norm, which is exactly what we would get if we all stop worrying about what others think of us.

For example, Singaporeans may suffer from an excess of conformity, which hinders creativity, but Argentines, Greeks, and Neapolitans suffer from institutionalized rule-breaking, thus downgrading creativity to a mere adaptational necessity. *Because* rules don't work, you have to permanently rely on your creativity, even for the most basic and mundane activities (e.g., parking your car, filing your tax return, or trying to stand in line). In anarchic cultures, if you are *not* breaking the rules, then you are an outlier or exception, to the point of being ostracized or made fun of because you are one of the very few people following the rules. Since most people don't, garbage lies uncollected on the street, taxes are unpaid, and institutions decay and malfunction. A Singaporean may have more trouble adjusting to Argentina than an Argentine would to Singapore, if only because of the Argentine's ability to pretend to adapt.

Selfish acts entail ignoring other people's disapproval or condemnation, and result in something that is at best beneficial to the selfish person, but detrimental to everybody else. This is not to deny the fact that rule breakers can bring about progress when they defy crooked or inept rules in order to institute moral or social improvements, or replace an evil status quo with something that improves things. Civil right movements, gender equality initiatives, and anti-Apartheid movements are all examples of defiant assaults on the status quo that had to overcome conformity and obedience. The same could have happened if there was an effective anti-Nazi movement in Germany to stop Hitler, who rose via democratic means, from gaining power. However, you need skills to break the rules, and even more skills to convince people that your idea of a better alternative truly represents the way forward. None of this can be achieved if you ignore what others think of you.

There is a defiant part in all of us that aspires to non-conformity, but is itself a product of our ability to conform most of the time. Take children, for example: If you want them to develop a healthy sense of rebelliousness, then be sure to instill proper rules, be at least somewhat strict, and give them a modicum of norms and structure. Out of structure, a productive sense of chaos and anarchy may arise, which could even end up translating into creativity, if not progress. But if you only give them chaos, or deprive them of rules and structure, they will instead crave order and discipline. And if they don't, they will just fail to adjust to the world. In order to break the rules, you must be deeply aware of them (simply knowing them is not enough). This also highlights the good news: It is entirely possible to find a balance between taking into account what people think and want on the one hand, and not being a total suck-up or conformist sheep on the other. In fact, the world genuinely welcomes imaginative acts of rebellion that also serve as acts of leadership and challenge the past (or even the present), while addressing collective dissatisfaction and exposing the obsolescence of ideas, ideals, morality, and the status quo. But—and this is a significant but—to be truly effective, you must not only acknowledge the rules of the game; you must master them as well. Only then can you credibly challenge those rules, and propose a viable "how" for doing things better.

Picasso's point about the relative ease with which he could master Raphael in four years, vis-à-vis the difficulties of forgetting to paint according to learned convention and habit, exemplifies the unnatural process of unlearning social norms once they have been acquired. Humans are very good at learning, but very bad at unlearning, so any demand to be authentic, by ignoring what others think of us, must take us back to our primitive infancy—to the naive past of our uncorrupted souls, and an immature stage of pre-socialization in which the creative act is admired, but only because there is no other choice except to create (since we have not yet learned to replicate, repeat, adhere, etc.).[2]

There is a well-established literature and an extensive body of research on the determinants of creative achievement, including the fundamental workings of the creative process, as well as the arduous and tricky passage from creative inception to practical innovations (i.e., from the initial emergence of creativity all the way to its recognition by others and actually having an impact).[3] One of the overarching lessons of this research is that authenticity is at best necessary, but by no means sufficient for valuable innovations to occur. Necessary, because almost every innovation starts as an act of originality, and because creativity is defined as the production of ideas that are original *and* useful.[4] In particular, the originality part of this equation (more so than the useful part) benefits from unconstrained thinking, freedom of ideas, and something along the lines of a near stream of consciousness or free association uninhibited by social rules and constraints—this describes the process of many creative thinkers and writers, such as James Joyce, Virginia Woolf, and Sigmund Freud, who made free association a critical technique of his psychotherapy approach. Unsurprisingly, this creative process is often lubricated by psychopharmacological or psychotropic substances, ranging from coffee to alcohol and other legal and illegal drugs.

It is in the lessening of mental blocks and barriers—and the transposing of consciousness from the mundane to the clandestine, or the superego to the id—that creativity may knock on our doors. In our wild and crazy moments, we resign to what we are in order to become what we want to be, but this is usually not what *others* want us to become . . . While there's something poetic about this unshackling of human imagination during the creative process, in the vast majority of cases, original ideation and unconventional thinking are unlikely to result in outstanding innovations.

Eric Schmidt, the former chairman of Google, broke down business innovation as being merely 4 percent dependent on the idea, while the remaining 96 percent was hard work, strong leadership, and a culture conducive to innovation. In the arts, we usually hear that it's 1 percent creativity and 99 percent perspiration. In science, well, the process, protocol, and method are so strict and dominant that there is little room for disruptive thinking at all—consider that Albert Einstein's masterful Nobel Prize-winning work was all but ignored for sixteen years. And in all fields, privilege, politics, hard work, timing, and luck are necessary to solidify creative ideas into actual, tangible innovations. You may be yourself in front of your social media page and that bottle of wine at 2 a.m. when you are alone at your desk, but the work that begins at 6 a.m. the next day requires you to recover your professional self and at least *pretend* to follow the rules you would so much love to break.

To be convincing to others, you must make your genius stand out by disguising all the processes, efforts, politics, and compromises that actually made it stand out—since even creative performance is talent minus effort; namely, the less effort you appear to make, the more others will admire your talent! Importantly, if you are seriously uncompromising and über-protective about your ideas, then good luck getting anyone on your side. Whether in business, art, or science, negotiation is part of the creative process, and it requires a great deal of editing and self-editing. There's a reason why "social capital," which is often a euphemism for nepotism or privilege, plays such a critical role in shaping individuals' and organizations' success, including their innovation prospects—"contacts mean contracts" as the old adage says, and contacts are all about perpetuating existing power dynamics and the privileges of the elite.[5] So, while talent and effort, not to mention luck, can make a big difference in your career, even all those factors combined will go to waste if you don't care at all about what others think of you.

The Perils of Low Empathy

Empathy—the ability to understand and care about the feelings of other human beings—is a fundamental component of healthy social interactions. The more people display it, the more you will enjoy interacting with them. The rule also applies to you. Your ability to display empathy increases your likability, and when you feel you cannot give a damn about someone, decide to ignore their views and opinions, or refrain from understanding how they see the world, they will gladly reciprocate those feelings. The development of a strong moral character enables highly functioning and emotionally mature adults to consider the needs and interests of other people, and adjust their own behaviors in order to avoid negatively affecting others. This means exercising high levels of self-control, modulating behavior to display empathic concern, resisting short-term selfish impulses, and accommodating others rather than hoping that others will adapt to you.[6]

Jean Piaget, an eminent developmental psychologist, devoted a lifetime to studying how children evolve to understand the world around them, a cornerstone of their intellectual and emotional maturity.[7] Around the age of seven, children start to give consistent signs that they are able to see the world from another person's perspectives, overcoming the noticeable egocentrism that governs their thinking in earlier years. In essence, normal humans evolve from being self-centered, and viewing the world only from their own point of view, to acquiring the ability to interpret things from someone else's vantage point. One of the famous experiments Piaget conducted to demonstrate egocentrism was the "Three Mountains Task."[8] In this experiment, children are asked "what a doll would see" when looking at a mountain scene from various angles. Younger children typically fail to accurately describe what the doll would see if it were different from their own view, showing their difficulty in understanding other-centric perspectives. As Piaget demonstrated, seeing things from someone else's perspective is a precondition to develop the capacity for abstract reasoning, which typically involves operating with principles and rules that are independent of our own situation, preferences, or state—and certainly of our internal wishes, cravings, and impulses.

As Jennifer Jason Leigh's character, Lorraine Lyon, alludes to in one of the most iconic scenes from the fifth season of *Fargo*, in which she confronts the tyrannical, megalomaniacal, and self-centered Sheriff Roy Tillman, played by John Hamm, the only people who can rightly aspire to having absolute freedom without any responsibilities are babies. Sadly, there are many examples of adults, including those in very powerful positions, who appear to behave like babies in this precise way. But just because they may use their power and status to get away with such behaviors, it doesn't mean they are a role model to emulate.

To be sure, the degree to which people care about what others think of them appears to decline as they accrue more status and power, to everyone else's detriment. For example, would Harvey Weinstein, Jeffrey Epstein, Bill Cosby, Woody Allen, and Jimmy Savile not have done us all a favor if they had been more thoughtful and careful, not to mention concerned, about what others think of them? There is surely no sense that they believed they were engaging in moral behavior, so it was more of a case that they couldn't care less about others' views, because of their sense of invincibility—or the thought that they would never be found out, which is the same.

The notion that we could somehow benefit from ignoring other people's opinions of us is little more than a myth—not just in modern, but also ancient and primordial societies.[9] Working collaboratively with others, not to mention coexisting with other humans, requires you to pay attention to how they feel and think, and make an accurate reading of the informal or unwritten rules of interactions—politics, if you will. Putting your head down and ignoring others' needs, thoughts, or viewpoints is a recipe for disaster and will hurt your career, rather than unlocking your authentic self.[10]

If you want to find examples for the reverse (that is, people who somehow manage to grow up without being at all impacted or influenced by others), your best bet is to examine the world of feral children.[11] They are a well-known figure in literature and folklore going back to Ancient Roman times, who have supposedly been brought up by wild animals. These stories are more myth than reality, but there have indeed been documented cases of children who lived apart from human contact at a very young age, and displayed animal-like and subhuman behaviors as a result. One of the most famous cases is that of Amala and Kamala, who were discovered in India in the 1920s after allegedly being raised by wolves, although the authenticity of their story has been questioned.[12] While not quite as extreme as being raised by wolves, there are modern examples showing the consequences of extreme social deprivation.

For example, *The Wolfpack* is an eye-opening documentary that chronicles the lives of the Angulo brothers, a group of seven siblings who grew up in isolation from others, within the close confines of their family's small apartment in New York City, which they were rarely allowed to leave.[13] This was under the control of their paranoid father, who claimed to be protecting them, and who only allowed them to have just one form of contact with the outside world—TV and movies—thus resulting in a childhood devoid of social interactions apart from the close family. Consequently, movies became their escape, their education, and their way to understand a world they were hardly a part of. They would meticulously reenact scenes from their favorite films, creating costumes and props out of whatever materials they could find, as a means to express themselves and forge a connection to society at large. *The Wolfpack* reveals how, despite their unconventional upbringing and the lack of social skills that resulted from their isolation, the Angulo brothers' resilience and imagination helped them navigate and ultimately find their place in the world beyond the walls of their apartment.

The case of "idiot savants" is another example of highly rare and anomalous instances where people are not sufficiently influenced by what others think of them. The term is outdated and offensive, and was historically used to describe individuals with developmental disabilities who demonstrated extraordinary abilities in specific areas.[14] The contemporary and non-derogatory term, "savant syndrome," denotes a rare condition that occurs in individuals with autism spectrum disorder or other developmental disabilities. People diagnosed with savant syndrome often have exceptional skills in memory, arithmetic, music, or art.[15] A well-known example is Kim Peek, the real-life inspiration for Dustin Hoffman's character in the movie *Rain Man*, who, despite being socially and interpersonally impaired, possessed the gift of an extraordinary memory and the ability to recall information with the highest level of detail. For highly functioning, well-adjusted adults, the contrast couldn't be starker. Although they are generally devoid of any superior cognitive capabilities, this isn't a problem at all, for they care a great deal about how they are seen by others, understanding that this determines whether they are hired or fired for a job, how much they get paid, and how far they go in their careers.

To be sure, this comes with some downsides. For instance, if you care too much about what others think, you may engage in shameless political manipulation and deception, convincing people that you are something you are not. Conversely, you could be paralyzed by fear and anxiety, refraining from public speaking, taking on assignments, or applying for jobs. But the alternative, namely a world in which we do not care about what others think of us at all, would be simply dreadful. Even examples of blips—in which we temporarily let go of our inhibitions, only to have other people notice—highlight just how important it is to be on constant guard, to monitor people's views and opinions of us, and to be able to tweak our behaviors and comments accordingly.[16] Such examples are the cornerstone of lawsuits and the perennial focus of media stories highlighting the embarrassing costs of not caring about what others think of us, and revealing our real or hidden self. They include but are certainly not limited to: bankers confessing to deliberately selling junk bonds in the 2008 financial crisis; senators and prime ministers sexting embarrassing pictures to acquaintances; and Hollywood celebrities engaging in racist and sexist rants when they are stopped for drunk driving by the police. If you add pop stars, athletes, and corporate executives, the list would be long enough for an entire book on these career-ending gaffes and blips. And yes, in some instances, the career-ending aspect was only temporary, because of the privilege, power, and immunity these people enjoyed (more on this in chapter 7).

There's not much difficulty involved in mastering the art of not caring about what others think of you, including in relation to everyday work situations or high-stakes interactions with others. For instance, there is not much skill required for showing up at the office wearing your Zoom pajamas, ignoring your colleagues' requests for help, or expressing your true emotions with your clients and boss; rather than skill, these actions only require a thick skin (though not in a good way), and they more often reflect a lack of (social) skills.

The unedited and unfiltered you is so easily unleashed that it can be found on full display when you are tired and fed up, or had too many drinks at the Christmas party.[17] And regardless of how and where it is expressed, the unmodified version is always characterized by a lack of empathy, which has a simple causal explanation: It's only when you stop caring about others, and ignore how other people see you, that you can "dare" to behave in defiant, antisocial, and obnoxious ways.

This is usually a problem, but there are some creative workarounds. In England, the debauchery-prone office Christmas party (though current HR practices have sanitized this quite a bit) has a special place in the realm of authentic behavior, as it represents one of the only legitimate professional instances in the United Kingdom where it is okay to "let go" of your inhibitions. Participants are given license to exhibit their unfiltered self to others, and historically, there was also a guarantee that even the most outrageous acts would be celebrated by others. In fact, there's actually enormous pressure to be wild and let go of your inhibitions—to the point that if you are too buttoned-up, sober, or focused on "talking shop," this will decrease your social status. It's all part of an important cathartic ritual that makes up for the tremendous range of social inhibitions that Brits experience throughout the rest of the year in any social interaction. As the Oxford anthropologist Kate Fox brilliantly states in her masterful book about English society, "If it weren't for alcohol, the English wouldn't exist," pointing out that sober English culture is so introverted, formal, and inhibited, that in a sober England fertility rates would collapse.[18]

That being said, the Christmas party ritual in Britain exists precisely to maintain the dominant etiquette during the rest of the year—it keeps it alive precisely by offering an ephemeral exit, a cathartic way to release and relieve the cumulative pressure to behave in kind, polite, and considerate ways throughout the entire year. It is similar to other events where moderation is temporarily replaced with hedonism, such as Mardi Gras, Carnival, April Fools' Day, or the Jewish Purim festival. Importantly, introversion—much like social inhibitions or the capacity to control your impulses—is not a sign of antisocial or egotistical tendencies. On the contrary, it may simply capture a tendency to be shy or respectful of others in interpersonal settings, which can perfectly coexist with a deep desire to engage with others, as well as understand, attend to, and tolerate them. If you are an overconfident, attention-seeking extrovert, as narcissists are, you are far more likely to ignore other people and downgrade them to being merely your audience, all in order to take center stage and make the world revolve around you.[19]

Equally, letting others talk can be a sign that you are listening, precisely because you are interested in others, as opposed to having others be interested in you. As the next section shows, one of the major explanations for why people manage to largely ignore other people is that they have deficits in empathy. Indeed, ignoring what others think or feel is not a sign of toughness—let alone being a rebel talent, free spirit, or disruptive change agent—but rather an indicator of empathy deficits.[20] The less you focus on others, and the more disinterested you are in their well-being and suffering, the crueler and more obnoxious you are likely to be, at least in the eye of others.

As noted, when poor old Phineas Gage injured his brain, he lost all social inhibitions and became obnoxious. His mind no longer cared about what people thought of him, leading him to hurt others by sharing his unfiltered and uncensored thoughts and emotions. Likewise, alcohol and drug intoxication leads to social disinhibition and increases sensation-seeking, which includes an appetite for breaking the rules and engaging in unconventional and risky behavior.

If you think of the typical individual who is truly unbothered by what others think of him (statistically more likely to be male than female), to the point of making no effort to be rewarding to deal with, please others, and empathize with people, well, that is more or less a textbook definition of a psychopath.[21] Extreme versions of empathy deficits also underpin autism spectrum disorder.[22] Cambridge's Simon Baron-Cohen (the less famous cousin of Sasha Baron-Cohen, aka Borat, and one of the foremost academic authorities in neurodevelopmental disorders, neurodiversity, and empathy) produced a seminal work in this area, highlighting that people who are on the autism spectrum show developmental deficits in what is known as "theory of mind," which refers to the ability to attribute mental states, such as beliefs and intentions, to other people. Empathy and theory of mind are integral to effective communication and relationship-building; deficits in either one are mostly manifested in the form of impaired social skills. In fact, even if you wanted to convey your "true self," or what you deem the best version of you to others, it is clear that engaging in open and empathetic communication is a better strategy for doing so, rather than plainly ignoring what others think or them altogether, not least because it is a way to demonstrate consideration for the perspectives of others, via active listening, expressing ourselves clearly, and finding common ground.[23] Successful collaboration, teamwork, and building meaningful connections require social awareness, an understanding of others, and meeting people where they want to be met, if only for the purpose of boosting their understanding of you.[24]

Along those lines, the tendency to ignore what others make of you—like the belief in the notion that others should just make an effort and go out of their way to adjust to whatever you do and who you are—is more likely to indicate narcissistic entitlement, a trait defined by the tendency to hold "pervasive feelings of deservingness, specialness, and exaggerated expectations," rather than a positive independence of spirit.[25] Even if you are merely interested in understanding other people, rather than conforming to their views, you need to be less inwardly focused, pay attention to others, and display social curiosity to learn what other people think and feel. By definition, this is more likely to happen if you don't ignore others.[26]

Although empathy is a foundational driver of any functioning society, it isn't enough. In fact, empathy predisposes us to act in prosocial ways toward those who are like us, which in itself perpetuates bias. This is because empathy evolved to protect our next-of-kin, offspring, and genetic relatives. And for most of our evolutionary history, this was sufficient, since we mostly lived in small groups and there was not much else other than our genetic relatives. However, as we transition to living in wider societies, big cities, and now an interconnected and global world, we must demonstrate and display the ability to be nice to people who we *don't* empathize with, precisely because we see them as alien or "the other," which mostly includes people who feel or think differently about the values we embrace and adore. Going back to the previous chapter, the more we want to be true to our values, the harder it will be to get along with others who are different or think differently from us, because we become more rigid and intolerant.

As explained in chapter 2, when it comes to social interactions, sincerity is the exception rather than the norm. To be sure, a real friend may know when it's time to provide us with a much-needed reality check, and the priority is to tell us what we need, rather than want, to hear (especially when it may be what we need to hear). I recall a time in which one of my coworkers mentioned to us, her colleagues, that this other person in our office smelled really bad. She thought we would be helpful if we let him know that he had body odor issues, so he could take the necessary hygiene measures. The whole office, including myself, found this to be a very controversial suggestion.

Personally, I understood the underlying morality of her request, namely to be helpful to him (though admittedly, also to the rest of us, since it was clear to us all that the person smelled bad). The question here is not whether the decision to provide this constructive negative feedback was borne out of empathy—after all, what kind of friend would not help their friend make a better impression on others—but rather, whether it is more empathetic to say nothing, for we may hurt our colleague's feelings. To be sure, if our friend paid more attention to how others see—and smell—him, he would have washed more often. Or maybe he knows, but doesn't care? Either way, chances are nobody in life celebrates his reluctance to give a s--- about what others think of him, for he is just an inconsiderate or unaware person.

Becoming aware of your reputation is also the ideal way to develop "self-awareness," which is best understood as the agreement between our self-views and other people's views of us.[27] By definition, this requires you to pay as much attention to how others see you as to how you see yourself, since you can only become self-aware by understanding the role you play in your environments, how you impact others, and how others value you.[28] Rightly understood, then, self-awareness is ultimately "other"-awareness. In line with this idea, a great deal of systematic scientific research has examined the gap between self-estimates and others' estimates of ability, which can simply be assessed by asking people to rate themselves on various character traits, beliefs, or skills, and then getting a group of independent raters to provide their own assessments of the target person. Note the point of having many raters is to aggregate or average their views of the target, thus providing an outside perspective of the target's reputation.

Reputation Rules

The way to gain a good reputation is to endeavor
to be what you desire to appear.

—Socrates

Henry Thoreau once wrote that "what a man thinks of himself, that is which determines, or rather indicates, his fate."[29] Despite the poetic value of his statement, he was wrong—at least according to science. In reality, our self-views are largely inconsequential, particularly compared to what other people think of us. Consider the recent news story of a worker in Munich's modern art museum Pinakothek, who decided that if he could hang his own amateur art in the museum—among the real professional art pieces—visitors may finally discover his exquisite artistic talents. So he did, but instead of having his big breakthrough, the wannabe artist was promptly fired (and given a three-year ban) after his mediocre work was found out.

Tons of scientific research show that it is quite common for people to have reputational blind spots, in the sense of being unaware of how they are perceived by others.[30] In part, this is because others are not authentic when they give us feedback on our behavior, or when they tell us what they think of us. "That dress really looks good on you," "You are so funny," "It wasn't your fault," and "Don't worry, you did a great job" are just common examples of what people—especially our colleagues, friends, and relatives—do to ensure that we are not upset, that our ego isn't wounded, and that our self-esteem gets pampered.

Now, let's consider four stark realities about our reputation:

It's likely different from what you perceive: Generally, people are not fully conscious of their reputation. This is because they don't dedicate much attention to the opinions of others. When it comes to 360-degree evaluations, or multi-rater feedback, there's usually only a modest correlation between self-perception and others' ratings, but a higher agreement among others' ratings.

Notably, individuals who perform well are usually more cognizant of their reputation. This hints at the value of knowing others' perceptions of you. Contrary to the traditional idea of self-awareness being a deep, philosophical journey, a practical perspective of self-awareness is understanding how others perceive you, making it a concept rooted in social rather than personal consciousness.

You may not care about it enough: People typically only show partial interest in their reputation, enjoying positive feedback, while generally ignoring the negative. The human propensity for self-deception is particularly notorious, with men typically being more prone to this, but women being judged more harshly for it. Our brains are predisposed to dismissing unflattering details about ourselves, while amplifying even minimal praise. This tendency means we often serve as our own most effective cheerleaders, not because we're oblivious to our faults, but because we're the primary audience for our self-generated narratives. Consequently, we're hesitant to seek criticism and prefer the company of those who reinforce a more flattering image of us, even if it's not entirely sincere.

Altering it is not a sprint, but a marathon: Opinions about our reputation form quickly, but changing them requires significant time and effort. Once established, a reputation is hard to shake off, and altering it demands persistent commitment. The residues of our past reputation linger, as evident in the experiences of public figures who've undertaken massive efforts to transform their public image, but still contend with lingering perceptions. Similarly, organizations can pay dearly for public relations missteps, as no amount of positive initiatives can completely obscure past misdeeds. While it's challenging to rectify a negative reputation, even a stellar one can be destroyed in an instant, thus proving the fragile nature of public perception.

It's an invaluable indicator of your capability: In essence, your reputation is the currency of your talent. From professional accolades to public perceptions of your competence, your talent is essentially what others recognize it to be. Except for those rare instances of undiscovered or underrated individuals, your perceived talent usually falls short of your actual capabilities. There's little advantage in possessing more talent than people acknowledge, unless you can convince them otherwise. Hence, your reputation remains the ultimate yardstick of your talent and a significant factor in realizing your potential. The silver lining is that being aware of your reputation can enable you to leverage your potential by finding the right niche where your reputation becomes an asset.

Essentially, reputation mirrors personality, and talent is personality in the right place. Secure a position that suits the traits others attribute to you, and your likelihood of success increases. As Gordon Alport, one of the fathers of social psychology, noted, "One's reputation, whether false or true, cannot be hammered, hammered, hammered, into one's head without doing something to one's character," a quote that highlights the self-fulfilling effects of our reputation on our behavior and identity.[31] When we internalize how others see us, we change the way we think of ourselves, and in turn act according to others' perceptions of us.

As Taylor Swift noted when revisiting her childhood years as an aspiring artist in *Miss Americana*, "All I wanted is to be seen as good by others, to become the person others wanted me to become." To be sure, there is a cruel side to becoming the person others think we are or should become, namely that the negative views people have of us, including prejudiced attitudes, will shape our self-concept and self-esteem. But your reputation isn't fixed by ignoring or denying it, but by becoming aware of it and working hard to change it. You always have an advantage if you know what others think of you, compared to when you don't.

Trap 3

Reputation Is an Art

Though reputation is king, there's an important element of subtlety and socially skilled doses of deception underpinning a strong reputation, which, in fact, must include the ability to come across as someone who doesn't care *too much* about what others think of them. In other words, those who blatantly shape their reputations to conform to others' wishes and expectations may still be viewed more favorably than those who quite clearly don't give a damn about what others think of them (especially if their behaviors go hand in hand with this antisocial tendency). But they will likely be viewed with skepticism and distrust for seeming too inauthentic, like a politician who is focused solely on looking good and gaining the popular vote, without providing much substance, talent, and especially integrity.

It's that thin line that separates strong political skills from being a run-of-the-mill politician. As such, harnessing a strong reputation is partly about disguising the fact that you care deeply about others. Your actions must show that you take them into account and respect their values and point of view, but your subtle performative skills must make it all seem incredibly authentic and genuine. Think about it: While praises, flattery, and compliments are clearly preferable to negative feedback, rejection, and insults, if the praises, flattery, and compliments seem robotic, posed, or fake, you will assume that the authentic attitudes espoused toward you are potentially negative, and are in fact rejections and (silent) insults. Therefore, reputations improve not through being genuine and unfiltered, but through making your deep concern for others and what they think about you seem secondary to your seemingly profound appreciation of them.

When people consider the importance of reputations, they are likely to encounter a multifaceted and sometimes insurmountable set of viewpoints, which they would do well to attend to, ingest, and act upon.[32] The best way to upgrade your reputation is to start by understanding how people perceive you, and this requires internalizing a great deal of viewpoints, attitudes, and opinions about you, including from strangers.

The Power of First Impressions

They say you can't judge a book by its cover, but when it comes to humans, it is impossible to stop someone from making instant inferences about other people, irrespective of their specific purpose and whether they consciously do so or not. Indeed, people make inferences about our deepest character traits—such as whether we are warm, kind, powerful, or assertive—on the mere basis of our appearance.[33] Thus, there is no second time for a good first impression . . .

Studies have shown that even strangers are able to make accurate inferences about others based on minimal information, such as their appearance or image. For instance, when you show people pictures of real-life corporate leaders—such as executives in US firms—they are able to predict not only how successful these individuals are, but also how effective they are as leaders, such that ratings of leadership potential based on these strangers' pictures end up correlating with their firms' actual success level.[34] Equally, if we showed pictures of people to a group of strangers, and these strangers, who don't know anyone in the photographs, were asked to rate each person on traits like intelligence, integrity, trustworthiness, and curiosity, their instant and intuitive assessments would align pretty well with those people's actual scores on those traits.

It should be noted that the accuracy of these ratings has nothing to do with the target's authenticity, either in its self-rated or peer-rated form. In fact, the above character traits are more than enough to "guesstimate" the person's potential and performance with an accuracy level that compares to the estimates of people who know the person rather well. In other words, the mental model people build of your reputation is surprisingly immune to your desire to care (or not) about what people think of you, though once people know you and interact with you, they will see you as trustworthy if you come across as empathetic and considerate.

Even before you meet someone for the first time, you can assume they have some expectations about who you are and what you are like, or rather, what you will be like—understanding this is critical to making a good first impression. Needless to say, this means being highly oriented to what people think of you, and caring a great deal about it—which is the very opposite of the "ignore what others think of you" rule of authenticity.

Contrary to popular belief, first impressions are not just influenced by social stereotypes; they actually contain valid information about who we are, and predict our actual career success and social status attainment.[35] If we showed videos of you to a hundred people who never met you and don't know you, and we asked them to assess your personality, values, intelligence, and deepest character traits, 80 percent of them would agree on their inferences, even after a few minutes of video. And they turn out to be rather accurate, in the sense of predicting not just how future colleagues, bosses, employees, and friends will see you, but also your future job performance and career success.[36]

Needless to say, these inferences matter regardless of their accuracy, which can work to your benefit (or not). For instance, if you happen to be the target of others' prejudices, you will be disadvantaged and have to work hard to convince them that you are an outlier.

However, if you are the beneficiary of these biases, in the sense that they confer some class- or group-based virtues to you, you will end up with a default advantage, and would probably not want to convince them that they should abandon their positive inclination toward the group you belong to.

We cannot stop ourselves from judging others as soon as we see them, or even before we meet them for the first time—expectations will predispose us to be positively or negatively inclined toward them prior to peripheral factors and adjacent experiences.[37] As research shows, even small children make instant evaluations and inferences of other people's character traits, including their competence and trustworthiness.[38] These come from effectively internalizing what adults teach them about others, consciously or not (an area called *social perception*).[39] There is a surprisingly high correlation between evaluations of our character made by strangers who barely know us and are guided simply by first impressions, and those by people who know us quite well.[40] In other words, it takes it takes strangers merely a few minutes to predict our personality in much the same way as our friends would describe it.

Just as we learn to categorize things in the world as *big*, *small*, *blue*, *red*, *good*, or *bad*, we also learn to classify them as *male*, *female*, *strange*, *normal*, *pretty*, or *ugly*. We carry these schemas throughout our life, and while we will learn many new things, we will generally struggle to unlearn things.[41] Unconscious bias training, which basically tries to erase people's stereotypes and make them overcome their prejudices, delivers little in the form of results.[42] For instance, no matter how open-minded and well-intended hiring managers or recruiters may be (or *think* they are), they will find it impossible to ignore that the person in front of them looks female, young, trustworthy, unreliable, and so on. In fact, the more conscious attention we may exert to ignore any of these demographic categories, the less we will be able to ignore it—"must not think she is a female, must not think she is a female"—similar to the famous white bear thought-suppression experiment in which people are instructed to think of anything they want, except a white bear, and they end up unable to think of anything but a white bear.[43]

It is also customary in any culture to pretend that we don't judge others based on their appearance, or on touchy demographic categories (e.g., race, gender, age, disabilities, and social class), especially among educated, well-meaning, and self-proclaimed open-minded and moral people. At times, this is because people are aware of the undesirable image they would convey if they admitted to judging others based on appearance, which would earn them labels like narrow-minded or prejudiced. Other times, it's because they would have to convince themselves that this is true, that they are sexist, ageist, classist, racist, and so on—time to go back to bullsh--ting others instead of bullsh--ting yourself. Ironically, knowing that you are guilty of judging others on first impressions can help you pretend that you don't, but truly believing that you don't may convince others that this is true! The sadly overused lines, "I am not a racist, but . . ." or "I am not homophobic; I even have a gay friend . . ." are more likely signaling effective self-deception, rather than successful attempts to deceive others.[44]

People's interest in inferring or deciphering our character traits also include their efforts to assess whether we are being authentic or not, with research showing that high levels of variability in facial expressions—think of it as the opposite of the Queen of England—are associated with perceptions of authenticity.[45] Again, it's not how authentic you feel, but how authentic you are in the eyes of others that matters.[46] This is arguably the biggest argument against the notion that we should just ignore what others think of us, especially if we care about authenticity. You must know your audience if you want to influence them.

Inferences about people's psychological qualities are far less reliable when what we want to observe is not directly observable, which is the case with authenticity.[47] What we may observe is whether people act consistently over time, but this could be a sign of both high or low authenticity. For instance, telling everybody the same story about some aspects of your personal life may increase the trustworthiness of that story and enhance your reputation for being authentic; but if you tell everybody you meet that they are the most special and important person in your life, your flattery and ingratiation will have little credibility.

Likewise, if you happen to interact with someone (e.g., a waitress, barman, shop assistant, or flight attendant) for the first time, and they seem quite charming in that they say nice things to you, then you may be inclined to think they are authentic. However, this will change if you overhear them say the same things to the next person. So, consistency may be a sign of authenticity, or lack thereof.

Toward a More Diluted or Sweetened Version of You

To be sure, there are many benefits to being *perceived* as authentic at work, just as it is clearly detrimental to be perceived as an impostor. Research shows that employees who are perceived as more authentic are more likely to gain acceptance into their colleagues' social networks, at least in organizations that aren't overly political.[48] However, the kind of authenticity other people value in you or others is heavily diluted by prosocial skills, considerate and cordial orientation toward others, and a strong dose of empathy. "Raw" authenticity, in the sense of not worrying about what people think of you, is too strong and too much for people to take.

While you may want to be regarded as authentic, remember that the real ingredients others want in your demeanor and style have more to do with social and interpersonal skills, including the ability to show empathy and attention to others, while coming across as genuine. When your colleagues request your honest feedback on their performance, insisting that you should really speak candidly, what they expect (and hope) is that you actually praise them, and only after you do that sufficiently will they accept a little bit of criticism or negative feedback.

Let's use coffee drinkers as an example: Most people love their sweetened venti cappuccinos and Frappuccinos because they are not really strong coffee lovers—the single espresso shot in those beverages is heavily diluted by milk, sugar, and extra syrup. Think of authenticity in the same way: It should come in small doses, making up just 10 to 20 percent of your comments, reactions, feedback, or behavior, so as not to result in a bitter, indigestible reputation.

We are in the eyes of others. We exist in their minds. Our reputation is not just owned by them, but constructed and maintained by them. That said, we don't play a passive role when it comes to shaping it or at least providing the raw ingredients needed to construct it. In fact, our behaviors, actions, and habits—especially the things we do differently from others, and contribute to our personal brand—are what influence and direct the shape and form of our reputation.

So, just like the choice on how to behave will help shape how others see you, caring about how others see you will be critical for helping you refine your choices and shape your reputation. Even if your goal were to come across as authentic, you would need to pay a great deal of attention to whether others see you as authentic when you say and do certain things. So, ironically, you earn the authentic accolade by worrying a great deal about what others think of you. The reason for this is largely due to the fact that if you stop worrying about them, your raw authenticity will likely be interpreted as a lack of social skills, interest in others, or sheer rudeness. Consider people who won't stop talking and talking, usually about themselves, and cannot refrain from mansplaining things. Well, they are the emblematic case study of someone who does not worry about what others think of them—or if they do, they are just not competent enough at getting the signals . . .

As one would expect, there are also some other sources of reputational influence that we have less control over, such as the demographic categories we belong to. For instance, people will make reputational inferences and construct a model of who we are based on whether we are young or old, male or female, foreign or local, German or Nigerian, black or white, and so on. And most people will feel no inclination or motivation to disregard the impact of these factors when it comes to working out who we are as an individual or person. Still, it is in our hands to act in ways that either confirm or suppress the influence of these social stereotypes on our reputation, and we will always have an advantage if we are aware of them, and of how they influence others' perceptions of us. For example, you go on a first date with someone and they ask you what you do for a living— regardless of who they are, they will likely extrapolate your personality from your occupation, including your proclivity to be more or less authentic. "I am a manager at Goldman Sachs" may receive a lower authenticity score than "I am an artist," even if this inference is totally unfounded. But an awareness of what others may infer about you based on common social stereotypes will help you refute it, or at least persuade your audience that you are an exception to the rule.

The same is true for nationality: Telling someone that you are from Brazil may nudge them to think that you are more spontaneous, authentic, and free-spirited than if you were from, say, Japan, Germany, or Singapore. This could work in your favor if you are going on a date, but against you during a job interview. And yet again, it is only by being aware of the potential influence of this stereotype on your audience that you can increase your chances of shaping their perception of you, and thus act in ways that are stereotype-defying (assuming this is what you want).

In short, it is significantly more advantageous to be aware of the stereotypes people use to infer your personality, including your authenticity, rather than to ignore them. It is precisely knowing what people think of you that enables you to persuade them to think in the way you want. If social skills are broadly about getting people to see you as you would like to be seen, and as you like to see yourself on a good day, then this is largely enabled by your ability to diagnose the baseline or default view someone has on you. Perceptions may be true or false, but if you want to change them, it is helpful to know what they are.[49]

Needless to say, cultures differ in their apparent "demands" for authenticity: As a general rule, the more authentic we assume people are in a culture (whether it be national or corporate), the more of an effort they need to make to avoid coming across as fake ... which again, requires a great deal of attention to how other people see you. In my own country of origin, Argentina, there is a big social "tax," or sanction, on people who seem fake. This doesn't mean that everyone is 100 percent genuine, transparent, or unfiltered when they interact with others. Rather, it means that when you praise, compliment, and "BS" others, you need to make a greater effort to come across as real. It is therefore no surprise that the main skill we Argentines perfected is not authenticity, but deception. Deception is also applied to coming across as authentic, which of course is key to enable further deception. Conversely, and relatively speaking, Israeli, German, Dutch, and Norwegian culture may be more "direct" and therefore authentic, which is why they are not stereotypically associated with kind, considerate, and empathetic behaviors, but rather with a preference for "getting s--- done," as opposed to being nice or charming to others. Same goes for New York versus Toronto, the Midwest, Auckland, New Zealand, and so on . . .

It is not just people's perception of your authenticity that matters, but their views on any impactful or relevant traits. Take trust, which, as seen in the previous chapter, is the lubricant that makes any society possible. Trust is not an inherent quality, but a hallmark of your reputation. You may think or feel that you are the most ethical, reliable, and honest person in the world, but what matters most is how trustworthy *others* think you are. What impacts how trustworthy people think you are? Mostly, your ability to behave in consistent, reliable, and predictable ways, as well as your tendency to prioritize others over and above you. The more agreeable, conscientious, and emotionally stable you are—which tends to translate into other-oriented, empathetic, and cordial behavior—the more people will trust you.[50] To be sure, trusting people doesn't always end well. There are plenty of instances where we trust the wrong person. But it tends to be because we follow or believe people with a very different type of profile—psychopathic, narcissistic, Machiavellian charlatans . . . who seduce us through their charm and charisma.[51] We often dismiss or make fun of people who flex to be nice, adjust their behavior to the situation, and care about making an impression on others, as if they were fraudulent phony losers, but we are far better off trusting these inauthentic people than a charming or charismatic bullsh--ter who is more or less holding up a sign, hiding in plain sight, saying, "Do not trust me, I'm a psychopath."[52]

There are multiple ways of becoming aware of what others think of you, a process known as "baselining our reputation." The process involves internalizing the beliefs, perceptions, and opinions people have of you, being particularly open to the different views different people may have, and attending to both their unique and shared opinions of you. Typically, the opinions that carry most weight are those of people who have frequent or regular interactions with you, because they have access to the widest range of data points on how you behave and what you do and say, especially compared to other people in those same situations.

The importance of sending the right signal to others, and caring about how they perceive us, is also underscored by studies into how observers and raters decode verbal and non-verbal communication signs, and the fact that people who are interpersonally effective and socially appreciated make refined uses of language and communication.[53] Indeed, everyday uses of language and communication show that we should care a great deal about what others think of us, even when we are not running in political elections or trying to get our colleagues to support our promotion at work. Verbal etiquette, code, small talk, and reading between the lines all evolved to enable this successful transmission between the sender and receiver of a message, which of course is central to professional and social cooperation among humans.

All nations have code terms in their language and interactions, so as to minimize negative reactions from others. If you inject some ambiguity and ambivalence in your communication, you stand a chance of being adequately interpreted *and* misinterpreted, which is a good excuse for when reactions are negative. Take Britain, a culture that goes to great lengths to finesse the art of double meaning, reading between the lines, and flexing language so as to say one thing, but almost always mean another. So much so, that you need to actually immerse yourself in their culture to get up to speed with the various ways and forms to express one's views and especially feelings, particularly when they are negative. For example, when someone tells you that your ideas are "interesting," what they really mean is that they are completely wacky, crazy, or off (sadly, during my first five years in the United Kingdom, I was convinced my ideas were really interesting, given how often people noted this); when someone says "I hear you," they really mean that you should shut up, and are trying to kill the discussion; when someone says that "you must come around for dinner soon," what they really mean is that they hope to never invite you over. Although the United States is more explicit and "active" aggressive, compared to the "passive" aggressive United Kingdom, it still indulges in double meaning, favoring oxymorons or reversals, especially to hide negatives within positives. So, "weaknesses" become "opportunities," "career transitioning" is the preferred term for letting someone go, "rightsizing" is a euphemism for "downsizing," and "poor culture-fit" is a vague universal excuse for rejecting unwanted candidates—like the "it's not you, it's me" line in a relationship breakup.

From high-stake performances (such as job interviews, client pitches, and critical work projects) to everyday interactions with others (such as the way we work, relax, and interact with others), our reputation is the working model of our personality that others use to make sense of our habits and predict what we are likely to do.[54] Note that when those "others" are individuals with sufficient power and influence to affect our future, it is quite irrelevant whether they are actually right in their views of us. This can work in our favor, when others think more highly of us than they should; or against us, when they underestimate our talents. Yet, we have a foolish tendency to assess the validity of other people's opinions of us by their closeness to our own opinions of ourselves, as if our self-views were the ultimate yardstick for our reputation. This egocentric approach to understanding who we are is an unconscious attempt to maintain a positive self-concept at the expense of coming to terms with reality. It leads to narcissistic and deluded self-views that widen the gap between our fantasized talents and the talents others think we have.

In situations that carry significant weight, such as professional evaluations or work interactions, our reputation serves as a model by which others gauge our behavior and predict our future actions. This model is important, especially when influential individuals are making judgments that could impact our prospects. Whether their assessment aligns with reality or not, it can work to our advantage if they overestimate us, or to our detriment if they underestimate us. Despite this, we often mistakenly use our own self-perception as the benchmark for our reputation, an inward-looking method that can inflate our sense of self and widen the discrepancy between our perceived and actual abilities.

In the end, the kind of authenticity others may tolerate is clearly not about being your raw, unfiltered self, but rather about projecting a version of yourself that resonates with others, while maintaining a semblance of genuineness. Think of it as a delicate dance where you blend social skills, empathy, and attention to others' perceptions with just enough authenticity to seem real without being overwhelming. We live in a world where our reputations are co-constructed by those around us. They hold the key to how we are perceived, yet we still play an active role in shaping that perception. The choices we make, the way we present ourselves, and even the stereotypes we navigate— all influence the reputational narrative others create about us. By caring about how others perceive us, we gain the tools to refine our actions and align their judgments with the version of ourselves we aspire to project.

Ironically, achieving the label of authentic requires a significant amount of effort to manage how others see you. Striking the right balance between authenticity and social finesse is the secret. Show enough of your genuine self to be credible, but temper it with empathy, social grace, and an awareness of context to avoid alienating others. Like coffee, authenticity is best served with just the right balance of boldness and sweetness, adapted to the palate of the person sipping it. By caring about what others think and paying attention to their perceptions, you can craft a reputation that's not only authentic, but also admired. And that's a recipe worth perfecting.

5

Trap 4

Bring Your Whole Self to Work

Under constant pressure to compete in the war for talent, organizations frequently offer "bringing your whole self to work" as a cultural perk, at least when they market their HR policies and cultures.[1] At times, this perk is defined by opportunities to "do what you love" or "express personal or private aspects of your identity" without the need to conform to rigid rules or cultural formalities. At other times, it is about slightly more superficial or trivial choices—like choosing how to dress during Zoom or analogue/3D meetings, or having the opportunity to bring your dog or your children to the office, which hopefully means your children can bring only their *best* rather than their whole self. But the goal is generally the same, namely, to include or embed nonprofessional aspects of your identity in your work (as it relates to time, space, and persona), so that "your whole self" is known to coworkers, bosses, subordinates, and even clients.

This recent HR obsession with wanting people to bring their whole self to work highlights the dominant corporate impetus to *negate* the existence of impression management, faking good, and inauthenticity (all three of which being the prevalent, if not ubiquitous, syntax underpinning interpersonal relations and exchanges at work). Alas, in too many cases, their promises are empty, a mere box-ticking exercise to *signal* that they care about workers' freedoms and their individual interests or identities, but without truly addressing their needs or upgrading their cultures.

Unsurprisingly, the workplace values professional demeanor over personal idiosyncrasies, and it's prudent to consider this in our self-expression at work. It is perhaps this very rarity of workplace authenticity that justifies repeated attempts to worship or glorify it. If the world had mostly authentic people, or the social or cultural norm was indeed authenticity, we would surely *beg* for inauthentic expressions of behavior! Like the "Thieves Will Be Prosecuted" sign in a store, or the "No Peeing" section of the swimming pool, you can assume that incessant calls for being authentic, like the never-ending calls for humble or ethical leaders, are just highlighting the fact that authenticity is an anomaly—we yearn for what is lacking, rather than what we have in abundance.

The promise of workplace authenticity reveals the tension between the ideals of freedom and individuality on the one hand, and the demands of professionalism and conformity on the other. While many organizations pay lip service to the idea that we are free to unleash our authentic or real, unconstrained self, the reality is that work, by its nature, requires compromise. Authenticity may be celebrated in theory, but in practice, it tends to succumb to the age-old requirement to "fit in," at least within reason. This also means that there are often white spaces for us to attempt to be ourselves, albeit in moderation.

The notion that we are free to somehow be ourselves at work is in stark contrast with the historical pressure, especially for customer-facing roles, to effectively manage our feelings, suppress problematic or negative thoughts in our interactions with others, and engage in emotional labor at work.[2] Indeed, despite the wide range of modern careers and the seemingly incessant increase of specific jobs and occupations (at the latest count, there were over 1,000 types of occupations in the United States alone), they all have one requirement in common—that employees adjust their behavior to satisfy the demands of their boss, employer, client, etc. Failure to do so will result in them not getting paid, or simply losing their job.

Note this is true even if you work for yourself and from home, where, admittedly, you may be tempted to feel that you are bringing your whole self to work—especially if you never change out of your pajamas and have your dog lying next to you, or if you live by yourself and have no one imposing a modicum of etiquette or self-presentation standards. At times, the primary concern may not even be whether our whole selves are truly invited to the office, but whether they are even welcome at home: after all, functioning effectively as a spouse, partner, parent, or family member does require making an effort to tame, edit, and censor undesirable elements of our self, as opposed to imposing our whole self on others.

Long before Zoom and other videoconference platforms became the most common substitute to the office, there was a visible trend for organizations to ensure more homelike or personal experiences at work. Most notably, as innovative Big Tech firms matured from start-ups to highly profitable corporations, they started turning their offices into adult Disney-like resorts or 5-star spas. The idea here was to create conditions to not just encourage employees to bring their whole self (including their childlike and playful social persona), but to also have them more or less live in and never leave the office. Toothbrushes were already included in the onboarding kits for big bank and law firm inductions in the 90s, but by going further and adding nap pods, sushi chefs, ping pong tables, and free laundry services, workers may experience such a massive downgrade when they return home (especially the small apartments that those very tech firms made extremely extensive to rent or buy), that they will thus experience a more meaningful or deeper connection to the office. This strategy blurs the lines between work and personal life, encouraging employees to live out a more aspirational version of themselves at work.

In some ways, this makes perfect sense. If workers are seeking out workplaces that value authenticity, companies are better off promoting themselves as organizations that value it. It's a talent acquisition strategy—similar to companies extolling their paid vacation, hybrid work, or work-life balance policies. There's also something more concerning about the command to bring our whole selves to work and to be fully immersed in our professional persona. Encouraging this kind of authenticity—even if it's not accepted in practice—tells workers that their identities must be intertwined with their job and career. It is something similar to the epitaphs of Ancient Romans, which were typically tied to their occupation: "Cornelius the baker," "Livia the farmer," "Lucius the gladiator," and so on.

Let's face it though, that's not how most of us think of work, let alone experience it. For most people, work is something they must do for others (e.g., customers, clients, coworkers, and bosses) in order to get paid, make ends meet, and pay the bills. If you love your job and career, that's great—but hopefully there's a little more to your life than work. And if you think your job sucks, and you have no spiritual or psychological connection with your employer, then I *really* hope there is more to your life than work! Luckily, despite the popular appeal of the "bring your whole self to work" mantra, for most workers it is still the case that there is much more to life than work, and much more to their identity than their professional self.

Not Defined by Work

Recent Pew data suggests that the percentage of people who see work as either a central, somewhat relevant, or totally irrelevant part of their identity is roughly the same—one-third in each group.[3] In other words, the majority of people don't think of work or their career as a critical part of who they are; it is simply not a defining feature of their character or identity, but rather something transient and peripheral.

Why? Well, because there are many sources of meaning outside work. To some, their most authentic self can be found in their hobbies, such as yoga, Pilates, cooking clubs, nightclubs, hiking, traveling, or stamp collecting. To others, it may be religion, community, family, or friends. And to others still, it may be art, music, or the aesthetic chills that emerge from contemplating an artistic masterpiece.[4]

Throughout our evolutionary history, and for many if not most people, work did not feature very highly in our sources of purpose and meaning—it was usually more of a chore and a necessity, one that we would happily avoid at the earliest convenience.[5] In contrast, modern knowledge workers seem to enjoy sharing their unsolicited views, values, and uncensored selves, including inappropriate self-disclosure, even when they are at work.[6] On social media, they feel compelled to share not just their professional updates, but their personal news as well—this includes professional networks like LinkedIn, where algorithms are optimized to promote the sharing of videos or photos where our broader self is on display, allowing others to experience more than our professional persona.

The dominant etiquette of the social media age nudges all of us to overshare, engage in shameless self-promotion, and publicize even the most private aspects of our lives to the world, albeit with a positive or optimistic filter.[7] Social media can be thought of as the modern version of Jerry Springer's eponymous show: On one hand, it appears to cater to our morbid curiosity for seeing the usually hidden reputational dimension of others; on the other hand, this appetite for the obscure and the genuine thus forces people to overdo the intimate, exaggerate the personal, and curate a personal self that is as artificial as any other public dimension of their reputation, precisely because they are catering to an audience. Put simply, something that stands out from the norm isn't necessarily authentic, and something that is normative or boring isn't necessarily inauthentic.

To be sure, there are limits to the degrees of authenticity we can tolerate in others, which underpins the current debate on freedom of speech versus censored or edited content, and was already a subject of much discussion during the rise of early reality shows, "shock TV" shows, and "trash TV" talk shows. As Oprah explained when asked if there was a difference between the kind of authenticity her own show pioneered and the more shocking or extreme version of Jerry Springer: "Confessing and baring your soul is one thing, but bearing your penis is another."

As such, it is hard to be sold on the idea that social media platforms connect us with other people's real or authentic selves, and in light of the digital narcissism that represents the dominant etiquette in such environments, one would hope that they don't. Indeed, for most people, the authentic self is the one that doesn't want to get out of bed on a Monday morning to go to work. This has always been the modern norm, with the exception being people who, perhaps because they got lucky embarking on their careers with some privileges or tailwinds, cannot wait to get into the office to experience a high sense of calling or spiritual fulfillment.

The fact that we have normalized the notion that we ought to "find ourselves" at work or in our careers is testimony to the strength of the authenticity cult—a propaganda machine that equates work to life, and sees careers as the ultimate source of meaning, purpose, and calling. Though far less discussed, let alone acknowledged, there are some very positive consequences to keeping your private and professional selves separate, and finding meaning in other areas of life. Burnout, work-family conflicts, and relationship problems are among the most common downsides of closely bridging home and work. In fact, there are significant individual differences that affect how people feel when their personal and professional identities are linked, with some personalities thriving, while others actually suffer.[8]

One of the advantages of *not* bringing your whole self to work is that you become far more resilient to professional setbacks and adversity. It is much easier to be laid off when you don't care about your job than when your entire identity depends on it. Likewise, not being promoted at work is much easier to stomach when you have a happy and rich social life, as well as many other entrepreneurial pursuits, than when all of your eggs are vested in that job or career.

Importantly, the assumption that people are naturally interested in bringing their whole self to work must also be tested against the rich diversity of various cultures and societies, where the rules of interaction are often markedly different. The degree to which employees may place value on identifying with their job, organization, and work persona is also to be considered, as there are known cultural differences in the value and meaning people assign to work and careers.[9] For example, the need to experience strong fit with one's job or organization tends to be stronger in the West than in the East, perhaps because of stronger individualistic tendencies in the West, which leave a vacuum of meaning and belonging for organizational cultures to fill. In contrast, in societies where relationships, tradition, spirituality, and family are a more prominent part of people's identity, less identification or connection to organizational culture is required for people to be happy or productive at work.

To be sure, the extent to which we need to identify with our employer is ultimately a matter of individual, rather than national, character or personality. In fact, even when the social norm is to worship and celebrate strong person-job or person-organization identification, we must allow for the not so unusual scenario in which people see work as simply work, and jobs as something to be done in order to have a more enjoyable life when we are not doing it.

Pressure to nudge people into seeking meaningful careers rather than just decent jobs may not alter how people think about work and the importance they attribute to their careers, nor is there any guarantee that they may find a job that is spiritually fulfilling, especially when they are prioritizing other things in life. We could even imagine that the pressure to connect emotionally and psychologically with your job may lead to feelings of guilt, shame, and self-criticism when you fail to achieve such connections, and thus make you hate your current job more.

Incidentally, being a great manager generally means understanding the degree to which *each* employee—as the unique individual that they are—is actually interested in sharing private aspects of their life with work colleagues, or expressing personal elements of their identity at work (rather than assuming everybody wants to do this, let alone pushing people to do it, especially because they seem to belong to a minority group or protected class). This will be discussed further in chapter 8.

Some Parts of You Are Best Kept Hidden

Whatever your employer tells you, parts of your *self* are best left at home, and don't automatically assume they are even welcome at home. Think of it this way: The average relationship would be

50 percent shorter if people expressed what they really thought and felt, and stopped worrying about what their partner thinks of them. Love is only possible because we are capable of hiding certain thoughts, ideas, and impulses—if you cannot control yourself and exercise some restraint, including self-censorship, and make an effort to be kind even when it requires a big effort, you will never be loved (unless you are a rock star, but then you may die prematurely).

In all seriousness, a very quick overview of the long-term predictors of romantic and relationship compatibility, durability, longevity, and success (however you want to define these) indicates one main consistent finding: Emotional stability, agreeableness, and conscientiousness—basically, the foundational components of EQ, or emotional intelligence—predict all positive relationship outcomes, mostly because they increase our proclivity toward respect, kindness, tolerance, and empathy, while being inversely related with passion, excitability, and volatility.[10] Work isn't much different than love. Putting others first and controlling your impulses makes for a long-lasting and happy relationship. The aim shouldn't be finding a group of people who will tolerate you; the goal should be to learn how to control the things that might put off others.

It is interesting that most of the pressure to encourage people to bring their whole self to work comes from the liberal left, or those who would be labeled as "woke" by those on the right. There is an obvious contradiction here: After all, being woke is about virtue signaling in an inauthentic way, or pretending to be more empathetic, caring about others, and embracing of diversity, more than you actually are. In other words, is the invitation to bring your whole self to work actually authentic, or is it like one of those faux polite British invites we make to colleagues and recent acquaintances—"You must come around soon" or "It would be great if you popped over for dinner when you can"—that aren't seriously meant?

When Apple hired Antonio García Martínez, the author of *Chaos Monkeys* and an active libertarian social media influencer, to join their firm as a senior leader based on an undisputed track record as an accomplished entrepreneur and executive, their workforce issued a letter to Apple indicating that they did not want to associate with someone whose values included preferring Trump to Obama, being against a strong government, and defending libertarian causes (inspired in part by Martínez's family history as anti-communist Cuban migrants to the United States).

Apple subsequently withdrew their offer and backtracked their decision to hire him. In essence, bringing your whole self to work may be okay if you fit in, but if you don't, we don't even want to see you at work? Same goes for Google's decision to fire James Damore for posting a memo criticizing their gender equality policies (which ironically was based on research showing a clear female advantage in certain areas, including leadership potential, and average deficits in others, such as engineering skills).[11] Certainly, Google's corporate mission to "organize the world's knowledge" is somewhat at odds with the decision to fire an employee for highlighting research that contradicts the company's HR policies.

The struggle at the organizational level is that it's always easier to manage people when they all think alike and fit in with others in the organization. If you run a cult, and you attract people who believe in the same things and have a strong, almost instinctual or spiritual connection with you, it is easy to persuade them to do what you like. This is why the organizational talk about authenticity often amounts to mere lip service—strong work cultures are usually built upon shared values, not unfettered self-expression. Though hiring managers may face pressure to recruit people who *add* to, rather than *fit* within, the culture, human nature gravitates toward similarity. It's always easier to hire candidates who reflect your own image (a socially legitimate way to express or unleash your own subliminal or unconscious narcissism). Just like it's easier to marry someone with your own values, personality, and appearance (ditto).

Yes, this tendency can be highly problematic. It can lead to group-think and leave those outside the dominant culture feeling marginalized.[12] If companies truly cared about diversity, they would incentivize managers to hire people who are their opposites and reward them for creating heterogeneous teams—not just in terms of demographics, but across values, styles, class, and abilities. It would be a great experiment in open-mindedness, forcing managers to hire people who are really incompatible with them in terms of thinking, values, and beliefs, but it probably wouldn't translate into team effectiveness. Teams require a *gel* that binds together its members. And that gel tends to be shared values.

. . .

In short, the notion of "bringing your whole self to work" is a tempting promise—an ideal that blends individuality, authenticity, and professional identity into one seamless whole. Yet, as this chapter illustrates, the workplace is not designed for unfettered self-expression, nor is it an invitation to display irrelevant or nonprofessional aspects of your identity, even when employers may explicitly request it. The demands of professionalism, conformity, and shared values usually override the lofty ideals of freedom and individuality that the mantra promotes.

While the idea of bringing your whole self to work may resonate as a marketing tool for talent acquisition, in practice it creates a complex tension. Encouraging employees to intertwine their identities with their work can blur boundaries and amplify vulnerabilities, leaving individuals exposed to greater disappointment and burnout.

The reality is that work, by its very nature, demands compromise, emotional labor, and adaptability.

Rather than striving to bring your entire self to work, a more sustainable approach might be to selectively bring parts of yourself that align with the environment and culture, while keeping other facets protected and nurtured outside of work. This selective authenticity not only safeguards personal resilience, but also ensures that professional relationships are built on respect, collaboration, and shared goals.

Ultimately, the promise of workplace authenticity may be best tempered with realism. We are all, to some extent, curating and managing the selves we present in any given context. The aim should not be to force conformity or encourage total self-disclosure, but rather to strike a balance that respects individuality while honoring the collective values that enable workplaces to function effectively. After all, some parts of yourself are best left at home (assuming they are even welcome there), not because they lack value, but because protecting them is an act of self-care.

Part Two

WHAT TO DO INSTEAD

6

Career
Advancement

Despite the near-universal promise of authenticity as a "magic bullet" for accelerating your career success, scientific evidence refutes this idea—regardless of whether we measure career success in objective or subjective terms.[1] The research evidence on this is quite unequivocal: Career success depends on doing the very opposite of "just being yourself." This is not to deny that some people may identify with their professional self once they have attained higher levels of career success, but the causal direction here is reversed. As chapter 7 will illustrate in greater detail, status and power do provide people with more freedom to "just be themselves," albeit to everyone else's peril. But, for everyone else, the rules could not be more different . . .

As we've seen, you're more likely to be successful if you

- Edit yourself in order to please rather than upset others, which includes the ability to be strategically *un*truthful with others in the interest of getting along and eliciting long-term trust (having a reputation for being reliable, safe, and trustworthy)

- Try to see things from the perspective of others, especially when they don't adhere to your values (which requires being largely focused on others rather than yourself)

- Learn to accept or at minimum tolerate other people's values, and at least entertain the possibility that your values may actually be wrong, based on self-serving and inaccurate beliefs, and at odds with other people's values

- Keep a watchful eye on what others think of you, especially when it makes you aware of negative views of your reputation, which is essential for fixing and upgrading it

- Sculpt or mold your work self so that it shows up as a sanitized, professional, and bright-side version of you, as often as possible, even when nobody (including your boss) is watching you!

These are some of the critical factors that determine and boost your career success, and they are the very opposite of what every definition of authenticity implies.

In line with these factors, there are objective generalizations to be made about the strategies that advance your ability to secure and retain desirable jobs, even if desirability is measured according to your own subjective standards. Let's take a look at some of these.

You Need to Play the Game

At key times—interviews, self-appraisals, performance reviews, and career discussions with your boss—you are tasked with advocating for yourself and your work. If you approach the major milestones or instances that significantly determine your career success with the assumption that you can be very honest, genuine, or authentic, you will be disadvantaged, not least since most of your competitors will be busy bragging, showing off, and taking credit for the things they did (and often for those they did not).

Furthermore, overly honest self-appraisals or critical self-evaluations—particularly those rooted in genuine self-reflection rather than self-deception—can work against you. The popular expression is that you might "hang yourself."

Managers tend to prefer to avoid conflict, so if you readily admit your shortcomings and tell them what you did wrong, you will make their job easier and earn yourself a lower rating—all they have to do is to agree with your poor self-evaluation. And they will rate you lower, especially compared to people who seemed so convinced of their high performance (even if illusory), that they will go to great lengths arguing with or confronting their managers if they don't receive a high rating.

When you are applying for jobs, authentic résumés or job applications might not convince hiring managers that you fit into their culture, company, vision, and purpose, not least because you will be competing against job seekers who are largely inauthentic in their exaggerated displays of enthusiasm for the particular culture of the employer.

The same goes for answering job interview questions, for example:

Question: "Do you enjoy working with others?"

> **Answer:** To be honest, it really depends ... There are times when I really feel a good connection with people, but I often struggle to collaborate with people who see things differently from me, or who cannot adjust to my own personal style. Perhaps this is why in my previous job I have not really been known to have the most positive team orientation, or for being the most collaborative person around ...

Question: "Why do you want to work for us?"

> Answer: Well, right now I would actually take *any* job that pays the bills. I don't know too much about your company, but the role seems interesting enough and I think I can do a decent job. I have been looking for something for a while now, so I'm open to different kinds of opportunities, including those that aren't a true passion for me. To tell you the truth, I am lowering my expectations and cannot be overly picky now.

Question: "Where do you see yourself in five years?"

> Answer: Hopefully in a job and company that I like, not having to work on stuff that I find boring, and making a good living without working too much. I am not really super ambitious in the sense of wanting a high-status career, or advancing to management levels. Basically, work is not the most important part of my life . . .

Question: "What is your biggest weakness?"

> Answer: I'm not really sure . . . I never really thought about this. I wouldn't even know what my biggest strengths are . . .

Despite the honesty, self-awareness, and unquestionable authenticity of the above (imaginary, and fortunately unrealistic) candidate, it would be surprising if they ended up with a job offer. To be sure, being at the other extreme of ambition, drive, and determination may also not be that helpful. I once interviewed someone who responded to the "where do you see yourself in five years" question (asked not by me, but the unimaginative hiring manager) by saying, "As the face of every $100 bill." Clearly 11 out of 10 in ambition, and perhaps also authenticity, but it hurt his chances. While it can be boring to be so formulaic, more often than not, the inauthentic and predictable candidates, who tell interviewers what they want to hear, end up getting the job.

Contrary to what you may think, the interview is not an assessment of how honest you are, but rather an invitation to show that you can play the game, that you won't be a high-risk recruit, and that, like the interviewers themselves, you are able to bullsh-- convincingly, either to others or yourself (and perhaps even enable them to bullsh-- themselves about the fact that you would be a great addition to their team, and that they have gotten to know you quite well, even during such a short and artificial interaction). In other words, the goal of your interview performance is not to display your authentic self or to answer honestly, but rather to *perform*, which means persuading others that you have the correct social skills to interpret what employers may want to hear, all of this while ensuring that your answer seems authentic.

Accordingly, interview questions will often probe into your personality, work habits, and compatibility with the company's culture.[2] So to play the game, you would need to respond in line with how other people would answer, particularly those considered a "good fit" or exemplary employees and leaders by virtue of their reputation as archetypes or emblems of the reigning or aspirational company culture. While coming across as honest is obviously preferable than the reverse—people want to feel you are being authentic, at least within reason—certain candid responses might not align with what employers are looking for in a potential candidate, or they might raise questions about your overall character ... even if you gain points for authenticity!

Consequently, when answering interview questions, presenting your experiences and traits positively while aligning with the employer's values can significantly enhance your chances of getting the job. Here are some socially desirable responses that demonstrate professionalism, adaptability, and a learning motivation:

Question: "Where do you see yourself in five years?"

> Desirable response: "In five years, I would really hope to see myself having grown both personally and professionally in a dynamic role like this one. I'm eager to take on more leadership responsibilities and contribute to innovative projects that align with the company's goals. I'm committed to lifelong learning and look forward to the opportunities for growth and development here."

Question: "Can you describe a time when you overcame a challenge at work?"

> Desirable response: "Certainly. Recently, my team was facing a tight deadline on a crucial project. We encountered unexpected setbacks that threatened our timeline. I took the initiative to reassess our workflow, delegate tasks more effectively, and stay late when necessary. By fostering open communication and encouraging the team, we were able to overcome the challenge and deliver the project on time. In addition to improving my reputation and trust with the team, this experience taught me valuable lessons in resilience, teamwork, and problem-solving."

Question: "How do you handle criticism?"

> Desirable response: "I tend to view criticism as a critical opportunity for growth. To be sure, it is not as comforting as praise, but it is much more useful and valuable in the long-term. I guess this is why I always try to listen openly and objectively to feedback, understanding that it can be hugely valuable to provide insights into how I can improve. While it's natural to initially feel

defensive, I've learned to take a step back, assess the validity of the feedback, and apply it constructively to my work and personal development. This approach has helped enhance my performance and strengthen my professional relationships."

Question: "What motivates you to do your best work?"

Desirable response: "What motivates me the most is knowing that my work has a meaningful impact on the team and contributes to the company's success. I'm driven by challenges that push me to innovate and improve. I find great satisfaction in solving problems, learning new skills, and achieving goals that align with the company's vision. The opportunity to work on projects that I'm passionate about and that make a difference is what excites me the most about coming to work every day."

Question: "How do you prioritize your tasks when everything seems urgent?"

Desirable response: "When faced with multiple urgent tasks, I start by quickly assessing the impact and deadlines of each task. I communicate openly with my team and supervisors to understand priorities and make informed decisions. I then create a structured plan, breaking down tasks into manageable steps and setting realistic deadlines. This approach allows me to stay focused and efficient, ensuring that I meet expectations and deliver quality work, even under pressure."

These responses demonstrate the ability to navigate workplace challenges with a positive attitude, a focus on solutions, and a commitment to contributing to the company's objectives. They "prove"—at least in the sense of convincing others—that you can put on a positive front and have a repertoire of socially desirable behaviors, that you can be rewarding to deal with, and that you can adhere to the appropriate cultural or social etiquette. Perhaps more importantly, they also show that you have the capacity to hide any undesirable qualities, emotions, and tendencies, which obviously means not displaying your whole or full self—only the good bits.

In essence, others will generally appreciate it when you display self-control in high-stakes situations, like a job interview, and keep any negative traits at bay. Consistency is key for them—between what you say and do, and between what you do across similar situations—as this will indicate trustworthiness. Other people will generally prefer not to be forced to constantly adjust their perception of you, which is mentally exhausting and psychologically tedious. So, it is not sufficient to have a repertoire consisting only of adequate social skills and desirable etiquette. You also need to display the same behavior time and time again, so that your acts seem not only authentic, but a natural and genuine feature of your personality and reputation. In essence, you want to persuade them that what they see is not the best version of you, but the typical version of you, so that they convince themselves that they will hire precisely the person they see, that what they see is what they will get.

Why Reputation Is King

Throughout most of our 300,000 years of evolutionary history, it was generally easy to make inferences about other people's talents and in turn make smart decisions when it came to assigning people to jobs and tasks, including leadership roles. There were two reasons for this. First, we mostly worked (and lived!) with the same small group of people all the time, so everybody knew each other very well. Second, the key talents or aspects of potential that we were interested in evaluating were largely easy to observe: skills related to hunting, fishing, running, motor coordination, and fighting, as well as psychological traits like courage, kindness, and risk monitoring. However, fast forward to our current times, and we are forced to evaluate very abstract traits, such as creativity, curiosity, strategic thinking, and self-awareness—even in people we never met or interacted with. This means modern organizations are often perplexed and confused in their quest for quantifying human potential and predicting whether someone will be good at an in-demand modern job (e.g., executing a digital transformation strategy or implementing a new-target operating model, as opposed to hunting a mammoth or helping their clan escape a wild predator like our forebears).

In an ideal world, organizations would be able to measure the potential of candidates more directly, without having to engage in this roleplaying and impression management exercise that is the interview.[3] In this ideal world, employers would also be capable of measuring the value employees will actually contribute to their organization after they are hired, in a very objective and accurate way. Career success would not be dictated by unfair access to opportunities, or by certain personal privileges that have little to do with one's contribution to the collective.[4] There would be no need to manage one's impression or reputation, take credit for the accomplishments of others, blame others for one's mistakes, or harness sophisticated deception techniques that trick others into thinking that you are better than you actually are.[5]

This utopian, idealistic world would be better for all, because when success and status are assigned on the basis of merit—and there is no gap between the value someone brings to a team or organization on the one hand, and to their own individual career success on the other—you incentivize people to work hard, give it their best, and develop the skills and talents that make things better, not just for their own personal career success, but also for others, including the wider organization. That is, you motivate people to direct and deploy their skills and work ethic in the interest of something other than themselves, such as adding value to customers, clients, and their employer's mission. Alas, in the real world, this happens only in moderation.[6]

In fact, the more you get paid for what you do, the more qualified and skilled you are, the more senior you are in an organization, and the fancier your job title, the harder it is to actually know for sure whether you are any good at your job or not! For example, we can objectively and reliably quantify how much value is added by an assembly line worker, an Uber driver, or a call center operator; but when we try to do this for management consultants, chief strategy officers, digital transformation ninjas, or chief happiness officers, it is a lot less clear. Granted, we can assign metrics or key performance indicators (KPIs) that are meaningful for the business, but they will typically be very detached and removed from the actual behaviors, decisions, and performance of these highly skilled and sought-after knowledge workers. So much so, that when a CEO tells us that their company increased profits, revenues, market cap, or productivity by X percent during their tenure, it is almost unavoidable to wonder: because of you, despite of you, or completely unrelatedly to you?

In the end, reputation rules, and your career success will be more dependent on your ability to shape it and finesse it, than on the work you actually put in, the value you create, or what you actually deliver. For this reason, when people say that they prefer to let their achievements speak for themselves, we must entertain the strong possibility that someone less competent (but less quiet, and far less modest) will be promoted ahead of them.

Be a Good Organizational Citizen

Nevertheless, we know a great deal about job performance, with a very sophisticated and established science devoted to it, stretching back over a century. This science tells us that a good way to define job performance is in terms of both task performance (e.g., productivity, output, results, etc.) and organizational citizenship (e.g., absence of antisocial behaviors toward others and the organization, presence of good camaraderie, ethical and prosocial behaviors, and basically being a decent member of the organization).

Although there are thousands of jobs, the personal qualities that improve someone's task performance are often the same as those that underpin organizational citizenship: being smart, which improves your learning speed and enhances your ability to understand formal rules (which is key for following those rules); having people skills, which enables you to work well with others, and to channel your ambition into positive team behaviors; and being driven, which increases your motivation, effort, and productivity. In other words, ability, likability, and drive are the simplest and most generalizable ways to conceptualize the essence of human potential. Whatever you need people to do, and wherever you need them to work, it is generally better if they possess thinking skills, people skills, and a strong work ethic.

And regardless of the specific job, role, or career in question, it is not just work, but also life in general that requires us to get along with others, and to engage in effective intragroup cooperation or co-ordination in order to get ahead of *other* teams and groups (i.e., effective intergroup competition).[7] Importantly, it's not about how smart, driven, or socially skilled *you* think you are, but rather how *others* think you are, particularly those who are in a position to influence your opportunities, choices, and possibilities (i.e., your boss and your boss's boss).

Performance thus gets translated into objective career success if you can convince others of the value you are adding, and of the fact that you are responsible for driving or delivering something valuable to a group or organization, contributing to the collective objectives. To be sure, at times the "value" you deliver may be largely indirect, such as helping your boss convince others that she or he is adding value to the organization, which in turn relies not only on their actual *performance* as managers or leaders (the formal role requirements focused on allocating tasks, monitoring others' performance, and directing the efforts of the team), but also how effectively these managers and leaders engage in the *performative* aspects of work, which largely involves managing their own reputation. In that sense, the study of successful people is by and large the study of people with successful reputations, or people who have been able to persuade others, especially those who have decision-making power over their success, that they are as good as they think, that they should stand out, that they are worthy of promotion, respect, and recognition, and that they are a valuable resource for the organization or society.

Now on to the good news: While the preceding paragraph may imply that success is rarely a marker of value or talent, but rather a prize unfairly given to professional conmen, tricksters, or politicians, this isn't so. In fact, more often than not, it's smart, driven, and socially skilled individuals who advance their careers. So much so, that the profile of high performers looks remarkably similar to that of successful employees.[8]

However, mistakes about people's competence are made, not least when their self-belief, confidence, and charisma are mistaken for actual competence, and those mistakes obviously harm the reputation of the organization in the long-term; the more often they happen, the greater the harm. To be sure, employees are not always aware of the value that other employees actually contribute to the system, and savvy employees will understand the importance of harnessing their reputations not just with their boss, but also with colleagues (peers and subordinates). Fundamentally, merit is an attribution, and whether you are worthy of your success or not is something other people will believe or not.

If you want people to accept that you deserve your level of success, you have to demonstrate it, convince them, be worthy of it in their eyes, and so on. There is no magic bullet to achieve this, but again, coming across as smart, likable, and driven will surely work better than the reverse. And of these three qualities, likability—which is encapsulated under the banner of social skills, people skills, or, more recently, emotional intelligence—is critical.

Emotional Intelligence, Redux

As we've discussed before, we'd be much better off if we strived to gain more emotional intelligence rather than chasing authenticity. But it's worth going into more detail on this.

People with high EQ scores tend to have an advantage in most jobs, careers, and interpersonal settings, primarily because they are more likable, rewarding to deal with, trustworthy, and resilient—all this, not according to themselves, but others. Therefore, the higher your EQ, the more likely it is that these related strengths are associated with your reputation in the eyes of others.

In particular, higher EQ signals a better capacity for self-awareness, self-control, empathy, and humility, regardless of whether these traits are natural strengths or whether people teach themselves to display them in critical environments—yes, the latter means faking them effectively, at least in a professional role or work persona. Furthermore, the ability to come across as genuine while you are engaging in successful impression management and socially desirable behaviors is the quintessential advantage conferred by EQ, and perhaps even the best and simplest interpretation of what EQ is in the first place.

In stark contrast with the notion that authentic people benefit from ignoring what others think of them, people with high EQ actually benefit from being acutely aware of what others see in them, and they frequently monitor how their own behavior impacts others. These benefits of EQ transcend jobs, roles, occupations, and contexts. In any culture, people tend to advance their career more, and unlock their potential, when they effectively incorporate feedback from others on their reputation and performance.[9] This enables higher-EQ individuals to achieve superior leadership performance (by knowing your limitations), display better social skills (by knowing what people think of you), and attain higher levels of career success (by knowing what you are good at).[10]

Further evidence of the EQ advantage at work is derived from studies of self-awareness, a key ingredient of EQ, which is also positively associated with mental health and well-being. When individuals have a realistic perception of themselves, they are less likely to experience anxiety and depression, and more likely to engage in healthy coping mechanisms.[11] Self-awareness also enables higher-EQ individuals to engage in better stress management, display stronger communication skills, and engage in more effective team dynamics. In essence, individuals who have a clear understanding of their own emotions and how they are perceived by others tend to navigate workplace challenges more effectively.[12]

These and hundreds of other studies demonstrate the wide-ranging benefits of EQ in both personal and professional contexts. By understanding how their self-perception aligns with others' perceptions, high-EQ individuals improve their performance, enhance their relationships, and achieve greater satisfaction and success in various aspects of their lives.

Note that high EQ doesn't just benefit those who have it, but also those who interact with them. That is, *because* they care so much about their own reputation, high-EQ individuals are more likely to help others and behave in prosocial ways. These effects represent a counterintuitive reversal of the mainstream understanding of interpersonal behavior: You don't help others because you are nice; rather, you are nice because you help others. In other words, the fact that you decide to help confers you with a reputation for niceness. So, our reputation is constructed and maintained through the behaviors we choose to display in order to influence people's perceptions of us, which include attributing certain traits, skills, and attitudes to our character or brand. And if the notion of helping others out of personal interest seems morally dubious, it is still surely better than *not* helping others or refraining from being kind or nice because you don't care about your reputation, or because you are "authentic." Just as fake politeness usually beats genuine rudeness, especially if you fake it well, benevolent actions spurred out of self-interest—the desire to be seen as nice—are usually preferable to antisocial actions stemming from of a lack of concern for one's image, or from a self-destructive etiquette. To be sure, it may even feel more comforting to assume that others are helping us out due to sheer altruism or because they truly want to do it, but this is a naive and childish approach to understanding the fundamental dynamics of work, where people get paid to not just produce, but also be nice or at least civil to others.

Importantly, high EQ is also associated with self-control, which includes the ability to tame or censor your dark side tendencies, undesirable habits, and counterproductive behaviors. Just as prosocial acts stem from a desire to make a good impression on others, antisocial acts (as well as a lack of prosocial acts) tend to arise from either an inability or an unwillingness to create a good impression on others, because we dismiss them or undermine their opinions. For example, self-control is crucial for helping you "let go" when your colleagues or boss annoys you, especially when you are convinced that you are right and they are wrong, which is the source of most arguments. If people had more self-control, they would find it easier to be nice rather than right (at least in our own view), and they would not have to deal with the painful sense of regret after falling out with meaningful others or upsetting those they actually care about, all in the interest of being right. In fact, self-control always plays a big role in enabling us to move from our actual self to our ideal self (our superego), or at least reduce the distance between them, thus becoming a better version of ourselves and upgrading our reputation with others, which is the only reputation that counts.

Furthermore, EQ is critical to the display of empathy, the ability to not just understand, but also care about other people's thoughts and emotions. Empathy enables pretty much any other-oriented behavior that contributes to a positive work culture and performance, such as showing strong commitment to team projects, having a positive attitude toward your coworkers and colleagues, and adhering to the existing group norms and rules so that team work is even possible. Anything of value is the result of successful cooperation and collaboration, and if you want to have an impact on others—either as a coworker, employee, or manager—you will need empathy to not just understand them, but also to persuade them to do what you want and see things the way you want. To be sure, power and coercion may force others to change their behavior, but if you want to change how they think or feel, you will need empathy to influence them. As Jonathan Haidt notes in his brilliant book on moral psychology: "If you really want to change someone's mind on a moral or political matter, you'll need to see things from that person's angle as well as your own. And if you do truly see it the other person's way—deeply and intuitively—you might even find your own mind opening in response. Empathy is an antidote to righteousness, although it's very difficult to empathize across a moral divide." Likewise, many decades before Haidt, the American industrialist Henry Ford noted that "if there is any one secret to success, it lies in the ability to get the other person's point of view and see things from their angle as well as your own."[13]

Needless to say, all things are best in moderation, and even kindness and empathy have a downside when taken too far. For instance, an epidemic of niceness or likeability—where people are so focused on getting along that they forget to get ahead—will plant the seeds of destruction in an organization wishing to remain competitive, results-oriented, and innovative. In smaller doses, we can see the same result when conformity, groupthink, and conflict avoidance become the default ways of interaction in a culture, thus extinguishing the much-needed diversity of opinions, tension, and drive that fuels innovation in groups, organizations, and societies. Much research shows that effective teams allow for a moderate dose of discord, dissatisfaction, and constructive non-conformity, which is enabled by having people with the "cojones" to speak up and disagree, and by having a significant proportion of the team *not* being focused on sucking up to their boss. Be that as it may, more often than not, and particularly at the individual level, it is better to be on the harmony rather than conflict side of the spectrum, and empathy should generally reign over and above self-centered drives or intragroup tension and conflict. Consider the fact that a seminal Harvard Business School study found that teams and organizations benefit much more from removing toxic workers than from hiring superstars.[14]

The EQ advantage at work, and yet another reminder of the inverse relationship between EQ and authenticity, can also be explained in terms of humility, which, like any desirable behavior, requires a great deal of method acting. Humility is one of those traits everyone claims to love, but few actually want to practice.[15] In other words, we love interacting with humble people more than making the effort to come across as humble with others. Research shows that humble people are seen as more trustworthy, better team players, and even more effective leaders.[16] Moreover, there is both a high cost to being perceived as arrogant (when your displays of confidence exceed or surpass your apparent competence), as well as substantial benefits to being perceived as humble (when your actual abilities seem to surpass your self-perceived or self-reported abilities).[17] That is reason enough to consider toning down the self-promotion—even if your inner ego is doing push-ups in the mirror. So, getting others to think of you as humble will boost your career success, but you will need to engage in a great deal of acting and performing (i.e., letting others talk so you can listen, taking into account what others, rather than you, want, and engaging in fake but realistic displays of modesty, including humble bragging). The more highly you think of yourself—especially likely if you deceive yourself into thinking that you are amazing, even when you are not—the more you should fake humility. Being internally secure can help you pretend that you are externally insecure or self-critical, which will get others to like you more, not least because they will assume that you are actually better than you think you are—even if this isn't true, but it is never really possible to be sure about this (and perceptions trump reality).

For the Folks with Low EQ

Despite the overwhelming evidence of the positive associations with EQ, this doesn't mean that low-EQ scorers are handicapped or doomed. For starters, correlations between EQ and all of the above, admittedly desirable outcomes and behaviors (humility, empathy, self-control, likability, and a positive work reputation in general), rarely exceed 0.3, which means that they overlap by only 9 percent. It also means that the valuable career and work outcomes impacted by EQ—e.g., team effectiveness, career satisfaction, leadership competence, etc.—are also determined by a wide range of other attributes, which are typically unrelated or even negatively related to EQ (for example, IQ, creativity, and drive). Alas, the diluted and distorted version of EQ that has been hijacked by the positive psychology movement has not just stigmatized and ostracized low-EQ scorers, but also created a bit of a witch hunt against people who, perhaps more authentically (the irony is hard to miss, since the positive psychology movement tends to champion authenticity), are more prone to expressing their negative emotions and feelings, more sensitive to stress and pressure, and more likely to adopt a pessimistic take on life (thus being more self-critical and prone to suffering from imposter syndrome).

The fact of the matter is that such individuals—who would typically score low on EQ assessments—may bring a much-needed dose of diversity to harmonious and happy teams, in which the focus is on getting along rather than getting ahead and winning. Creative people, who are the engine of innovation in any team, often display many qualities associated with lower EQ. For example, artistic moodiness, nonconformism, hostile impulsivity, and excitability ("up-and-down") are all found in those who possess a creative temperament, an entrepreneurial disposition, and a mindset for innovation. While it is of course possible for creative people to be emotionally intelligent, the more common pattern for high-EQ scorers is that they are better at following processes, building relations, and working with others, but to lack the necessary levels of non-conformity and unconventionality that can drive them to challenge the status quo and replace it with something new. Moreover, in complex and highly skilled jobs, including many scientific and technical fields, success is usually driven by one's ability to solve complex problems, innovate, and conduct detailed research, and top performers excel more through their intellectual (rather than emotional) intelligence. Individuals with lower EQ might thrive in these environments, especially if the job requires long hours of solitary work or highly specialized knowledge that doesn't rely on emotional communication or team collaboration, and where it is an asset to be overly alert to potential risks and threats, in the sense of having an adaptive level of pessimism and cynicism (e.g., corporate lawyers, cybersecurity analysts, air traffic controllers, etc.)

That said, in most settings, a lower EQ will make it even more imperative that you learn to master political skills and put on a fake repertoire of inauthentic behaviors that makes you more likeable, as well as less impulsive, irritable, high-maintenance, or intense. Same goes for creative jobs, since turning even the most brilliant creative ideas into actual innovations requires working well with others, as well as influencing, persuading, and getting people on board and excited by your vision.

It is also noteworthy that there are significant cultural differences in the degree to which these low-EQ, but highly authentic, behaviors will be tolerated, let alone accepted. This is an area where cultural stereotypes about preferred behavioral approaches and adaptions are often correct (though at the aggregate level, of course). For instance, if you behave like a passionate Argentine in cold Finland, you better make sure that people know that you are Argentine, so they can at least be more forgiving when it comes to reacting to your comparably intense, dramatic, and colorful displays of your authentic self, which will still require a great deal of tolerance and patience from the more restrained, coolheaded, and introverted Finns. Needless to say, if this Argentine is working in Finland, we would expect her to slowly but steadily adjust her behavior to learn to behave in more Finnish ways, which wouldn't compromise who they really are, but rather show-case an empathic, selfless, and socially skilled appreciation of the host culture.

Conversely, a Finnish person hoping to climb the career ladder in Argentina would benefit from some coaching to master the art of overcommunication, learning to fake or at least exaggerate displays of passion or enthusiasm, and, above all, learning to adapt and deal with more intensely passionate work colleagues than they would find at home. By the way, the more volatile nature of classic Argentine temperament is a sign of lower EQ, while the more *un*emotional nature of Finnish people is a classic indicator of high EQ.

Whatever culture you inhabit, if your EQ is low, there is generally a stronger case for harnessing the art of impression management to advance your career, in particular . . . learning to fake high EQ! You may call it self-coaching if you like, since most coaching is to some degree EQ coaching, but it's also pertinent to see this as training, which is really about building new habits as an attempt to create a reputation for having higher EQ. Dale Carnegie, one of the first and perhaps most famous self-help gurus, wrote extensively about this long before EQ was coined as a term. The realization that strong intrapersonal and interpersonal skills, as well as adherence to the dominant etiquette, are a better approach to improving one's career than unleashing one's unfiltered or authentic self on others, is far from new.

Sadly, many people assume that just because they are smart (or, worse, just *think* they are), they can be a pain in the ass. Equally, if you are extremely driven, ambitious, and goal oriented, you'd better have some people skills to be able to get along with others while you are focused on getting ahead—or you will be deemed pathologically ambitious, greedy, a team killer, etc.

The reality is that even people with limited ability and drive stay in their jobs a long time, and get promoted over their smart and driven counterparts, purely because they are rewarding to deal with, and manage to not annoy their colleagues and bosses. The reason is fairly easy to comprehend, namely that people who have the ability to exercise some power and decision-making over your career, including the options and alternatives that are available to you, will generally care about having pleasant interactions with you. If you are rewarding to deal with, others will want you around and help you out. If you are a pain in the ass, they will be delighted to ignore you, send you away as far as possible, or stand in the way between you and your career success.

Studies show that, so long as you are politically skilled, faking modesty, especially with your boss, is conducive to higher levels of career success.[18] Contrast this with the reverse, namely, conveying your honest or sincere arrogance to others at work, and telling colleagues and your boss how brilliant and talented you are, especially compared to others, including them! If for some reason you think this is a great idea, there's a significant chance you are in serious need of honest feedback from others—or perhaps they have been desperately trying to provide it to you, but gave up because you are immune to it.

Perhaps wishful thinking also plays a part, since observers would rather assume that others are acting authentically toward them, as if they were unable or unwilling to hide things from them. For instance, when you go to a restaurant and your waiter is being friendly, it is more comforting to assume that they truly like you and are behaving in a genuine and authentic way, than to think that they are engaging in professional displays of emotional labor, which would imply they are fake and therefore do not like us as much as it seems. Likewise, when the barman is acting like he is a close friend of mine, I will tip him more if I think he is genuinely being nice than if I believe he is just acting nice because wants my tip. In reality, there's no reason to be upset by the prospect that others are not being authentic or making an effort to adjust their behavior toward us. It is in fact quite the opposite: When others adjust their behavior because of our mere presence, it is a sign that they respect and care about us, or at least about the rules that facilitate and enable social interactions in civil society. And yet, we don't just want service with a smile, we want it to be a real or genuine smile. Likewise, we don't just want others to act nicely toward us, we want them to really mean it. We want our presence to evoke the legitimate desire to be authentic, as if we inspire this level of trust and safety. Interestingly, we no longer want this if it helps people express any negative feelings toward us. In other words, we expect others to be rewarding to deal with, to be happy, and to seem nice and friendly in a way that doesn't feel fake. However, if they are grumpy, unhappy, or annoyed, we would rather have them hide these emotions, to the point that we are not even aware that they are hiding them.

As noted earlier, it is more advantageous to fake humility than confidence, though there are stark cultural differences in our tendency to reward both. For example, Americans, Argentines, and Israelis are more accepting of self-promotion than other nations are, and they also tolerate self-deception more than other societies do—not least because it increases the impact of self-promotion. Although displaying high levels of self-confidence is a common presentation strategy in America—unlike, say, Sweden, Finland, Korea, or Japan—scientific evidence clearly suggests that the confidence surplus people perceive (i.e., surpassing your actual competence) can turn into a toxic asset. In other words, the minute people notice that you have more confidence than competence, your assertiveness will work against you—and, if they never actually notice, then it will work against *them*.

It's often observed that individuals who overtly promote themselves risk coming across as overconfident or presumptuous.[19] Respect and admiration are typically earned when one refrains from making boastful claims about their own abilities. Those who are genuinely skilled tend to stand out through their accomplishments, without having to highlight them vocally; such genuine talent is not commonplace, and not everyone is accustomed to encountering it. Masking one's own shortcomings and vulnerabilities can be done through grandstanding or, more subtly, by adopting a more humble and understated approach. In reality, only those with a poor understanding of true skill might confuse overt confidence with actual ability, and even then, it's often more effective to be liked for humility rather than disliked for vanity.

Therefore, if your skills are solid, there's no need to overstate them; conversely, pretending to be confident will not indefinitely cover up one's deficits and will only fool a few for so long. Moreover, when genuine ability is paired with humility and even a touch of self-doubt, it can not only impress, but also engender goodwill from others.

In general, our overly optimistic self-views cloud our probabilistic estimates of both good and bad future outcomes. For instance, when people are confronted with different expert opinions about their future health, finance, relationship, or career success, they overwhelmingly pick the most optimistic or rosy outcome. And, even when bad outcomes evidently occur for them, they persist in their wishful thinking, rather than improving their self-awareness. To cultivate self-awareness, you can develop a new habit: seeking feedback from others, and learning to internalize how they view you. As noted, our success is mostly determined by what other people think of us. So, even when they are wrong and hold inaccurate impressions of us, those impressions will have self-fulfilling consequential outcomes. Moreover, compared to our own self-estimates of personality, intelligence, and potential, others are not only better than us at estimating our character traits (including our work-related talent and potential), they are also better than us at predicting how we will perform.[20] Remember: It is not about how smart, driven, or likeable you are, but rather how others think you are. Even if you are not particularly inclined to care about what other people think of you, you may still be interested in making accurate predictions about your chances of success in different areas of life. As such, paying attention to other people's opinions of you, including their evaluations of your potential, is certainly useful.

In particular, getting negative or critical feedback from your co-workers—as opposed to only praises and compliments, especially when these are not authentic—fuels your personal and professional development.[21] This is why it is helpful to develop the social skills that help others provide us with constructive negative feedback on our performance, talent, and potential: "What would you do differently in my position?" "How would you have done this better?" "What are the two things that I can improve on?" All of these questions will nudge and prompt more sincere and useful feedback from others, compared to the classic, "Wasn't I great?"

It is precisely because most people are not antisocial or empathy-deprived (meaning they do care about what others think and feel) that they are often mindful of hurting our feelings, which they know is more likely to happen if they provide us with negative feedback—even when it is a constructive recommendation that may help us. As a result, we find ourselves in a catch-22 scenario where we are automatically tuned to ignore negative feedback and interpret things in an ego-syntonic way; and to top that off, others prefer to give us fake polite praises rather than constructive and honest criticism. Furthermore, even in the rare instances that they decide to provide us with the gift of well-intended negative feedback, the authenticity cult nudges us to ignore them, and to not worry about what others think of us, since we are as great as we think we are. In essence, we end up being completely shielded, if not immune, to negative feedback and criticism. How, then, could we not feel great about ourselves? How could we not think that we should be our own boss, that we deserve the best job in the world, and that other people should really admire our greatness? How could we not be the hero in our own mind, even if nobody else is watching that movie? And if there was any doubt, then we can always vote for presidents or elect heads of states that remind us that we are amazing and all our problems are someone else's fault, which they will deal with by making everything, and especially us, great (again). In this context, we should not be surprised that it is hard to know what others think of us, particularly the parts of us they don't like.

Therefore, even if you impress uninformed or amateur observers—who may experience a bit of FOMO from seeing you conduct yourself in this self-assured, anarchic, and disruptive way—there is little evidence for the notion that doing so will in any way signal actual talent or competence, which poses two big problems. The first is that you may end up believing your own hype, which undermines your ability to improve or actually develop skills. The second problem is that while this strategy may help you fool others, to the point of helping you advance your career, this will come at everybody's peril or expense. Wherever in the world you are reading this, I bet that you do not need to think very hard when it comes to finding examples of people who ascend to positions of power because of their confidence rather than competence, only to be found out when it is too late to remove them or remedy the damages they have done. Politics is of course the most emblematic example of this, but alas it happens in every organization, system, group, and part of society. In our minds, confidence may equate to competence 90 percent of the time; in reality, as systematic academic research shows, the overlap is closer to 10 percent.

Needless to say, the kind of confidence you may exude by ignoring others making polemical or antisocial comments during a work meeting, or by being politically incorrect when everybody is trying to be courteous and polite, is not something one should be proud of—and if you are, that will still not advance your career success, unless you are an aspiring populist politician, and you have the charisma to back it up. Unfortunately, charisma is often a sign of dark side traits, such as psychopathy.[22] This is why there are no shortage of examples of famous charismatic leaders who derail by turning their supporters and followers into victims, whether in politics, the corporate world, or any group in which leaders are elected or selected because of style rather than substance. When confidence trumps competence, we end up with incompetent leaders who have parasitic effects on their teams and organizations, thus contaminating cultures and societies (similar to bacteria contaminating other organisms).

This is not to dismiss the issue of caring so much about what others think of you that you become overly inhibited and self-censor yourself to the point that your performance anxiety, fear of failure, or negative evaluation apprehension handicaps you. But in reality, there are far fewer instances of this than we think, especially compared to the prevalence of the reserve case, namely people who are less inhibited by other people's opinion of them than they should. Indeed, for every person who self-censors, there are many more who would benefit from doing so, but are unwilling, if not ignorant of the benefits. That colleague who can't shut up during meetings, and doesn't get the signals from others to stop when he's mansplaining things; that boss who inadvertently says offensive or rude things, hurting the feelings and morale of her own team; and the many people who entertain us by auditioning for the *X Factor* reality show and mostly being selected for exhibiting an abysmal gap between their astronomic self-views and their diminutive talents (not to mention the fictional but hyperrealistic characters portrayed by Ricky Gervais and Steve Carell in *The Office*). It is not that there is a rarity of bosses who are kind, considerate, and able to think twice about what they say because they don't want to come across as obnoxious, but they generally make good bosses, which would make for rather boring comedy. Generally speaking, bosses are like referees: The less you notice them, the better they are; and the more likely it is that they are spending a great deal of time noticing you. Paradoxically, the less you care about your reputation, the more others will care, and not for good reasons!

Societies are well-oiled systems for interpersonal exchange where people are willing to adjust their behavior to make a positive impression on others. When they don't adjust, they stand out, and usually end up marginalized.

To be sure, the degree to which people are coerced to fit in varies from one society to the other, and it always comes with both costs and benefits. The Swedes say that the nail that sticks out must be hammered in, which, to Americans, smells like Soviet or communist conformity. However, there are still rules on how to fit in and behave in America, which is perhaps more tolerant of eccentricity than other nations, at least in theory. These rules are best noticed when we compare the etiquette of different American states. In Minnesota, for instance, the concept of "Minnesota nice" encapsulates the state's approach to etiquette, which emphasizes politeness, reserved behavior, and a tendency to avoid confrontation. In contrast, a typical New Yorker will be given quite a bit of license to engage in direct, aggressive, loud, and confrontational behavior—even if they are being friendly with you. In Kentucky, traditional Southern manners, such as referring to individuals with honorifics (Mr., Mrs., or Miss) and using "sir" or "ma'am," are still prevalent and expected. In Washington State, particularly in tech-forward Seattle, interactions are more casual, and first-name-basis greetings are common even in professional settings. These differences are not just a formality, they also influence the "power distance" in everyday interactions: non-hierarchical in Seattle, and more status-conscious and hierarchical in Kentucky. Likewise, whether you attend church, own guns, drive a big truck, or are a NASCAR fan, these are all defining features of your reputation, though less so if you live in places where such things are the norm, in which case *not* adhering to these habits will be your defining feature. Needless to say, allowing people to not fit in is still a rule, especially when you encourage or push them to do so. For instance, the pressure to just be yourself is no different from the pressure to *not* be yourself, especially when it involves internalizing a command from others. To be sure, the free-spirited aspect of the "don't worry about what others think of you" mantra would be more believable if it didn't itself originate from a command by, well, others.

Last but not least, there is a compelling case for simulating happiness, but it requires convincing others that you are happy even if you're not. The most obvious reason to simulate happiness is that it enhances your career progression, as most employers tend to prefer seeing you happy—regardless of whether this is a true reflection of your internal emotional state—rather than grumpy, especially if the latter includes putting up with your constant whining, complaining, and b-tching.

Showcasing your genuine misery to others will not advance your career as much as being able to fake happiness at work. Consider that a great deal of counterproductive work behaviors—including toxic gossiping, bullying, antisocial behaviors, theft, absenteeism, and underperformance—are largely caused by employees expressing, rather than repressing, their dissatisfaction at work. In contrast, studies indicate a positive correlation between the appearance of happiness and job performance, thus leading to higher chances for professional advancement. Managers often prefer the optimistic demeanor of employees, sometimes over more competent yet less cheerful individuals, due to the perception of emotional stability.

Sure, being truly happy with your career may be preferable, but it is often not a realistic possibility. Consider that the vast majority of workers in the world live in places where job markets, unemployment rates, upward social mobility, and overall career opportunities are far from ideal, and if you happen to have a job that doesn't make you absolutely miserable, you should consider yourself lucky. Incidentally, even in nations with greater economic prosperity, the vast majority of workers are disengaged or not engaged, meaning there's no indication that their jobs or careers elicit happiness. When a job causes misery, leaving might seem like the obvious solution, but this isn't always simple or feasible, especially when one's long-term goals are considered. Moreover, there's no guarantee that a new job will bring happiness. If authentic happiness is out of reach, then feigning contentment may be the next best strategy. This could be more beneficial than displaying genuine dissatisfaction, which may alienate colleagues and superiors.

Importantly, faking happiness will be particularly valuable not just if you are an employee, but also a manager or leader. Indeed, projecting happiness—and learning it to fake it in a convincing and believable way—can make you a more effective and successful leader. Emotional intelligence is highly valued in leadership, with happy-seeming leaders engaging more effectively with their teams. The qualities of happiness—stability, positivity, and resilience—are desired in leaders and can uplift the entire team's spirit. Think of it as the opposite of being a stress agent or major cause of anxiety for your team and organization because you are either unable or unwilling to control your negative emotions and refrain from communicating your stress, negativity, anger, or dissatisfaction to others. The next chapter discusses this, and other important ways in which leaders must ideally refrain from being authentic, in more detail.

. . .

Despite the pervasive mantra that authenticity is a career super-power, the evidence suggests otherwise. Success in the workplace is not about being your raw, unfiltered self, but about curating a professional version of yourself that aligns with expectations, social norms, and organizational goals. Whether you're navigating an interview, engaging in self-promotion, or managing workplace relationships, the ability to balance self-awareness with strategic self-presentation is critical.

This doesn't mean abandoning your values or deceiving others—it means understanding that career progression relies heavily on impression management, emotional intelligence, and adaptability. The workplace rewards those who can align their behaviors with shared goals, demonstrate likability and professionalism, and prioritize collaboration over unchecked individuality. In other words, your reputation, not your unvarnished self, is often the key driver of success.

The idea of "faking it" may sound disingenuous, but it's a fundamental aspect of navigating professional environments. By cultivating humility, managing emotional expressions, and projecting optimism—even when it feels unnatural—you can foster trust, build relationships, and create opportunities for growth. While it's tempting to idealize authenticity as a virtue, the reality is that a nuanced

and strategic approach to self-management often yields better results, both for you and for the teams and organizations you support.

In the end, success isn't about choosing between authenticity and
adaptability; it's about ensuring that your professional self comes
across as likable while seeming genuine. Sure, you can bring pieces of
your authentic self to work, but only when doing so enhances your
effectiveness and supports your professional goals. After all, the
world of work is less about "being yourself" and more about being
your *best self*—or at least the version of yourself that others are willing to bet on.

7

Leadership

> To be authentic means to be in touch with and express
> one's true feelings, and although that may sound good,
> it doesn't make sense. Leaders don't need to be true
> to themselves; in fact, being authentic is the opposite
> of what they should do.
>
> **—Jeffrey Pfeffer**

Few myths are as pervasive—and wrong—as the notion that leaders ought to be authentic. As Jeffrey Pfeffer, renowned Stanford professor and leadership expert, alludes in his book *Leadership BS*, the assumption that leaders ought to be authentic, in the sense of either expressing their true feelings or being true to themselves, is in direct contradiction to what effective or competent leadership looks like.[1]

The stark contrast highlighted by Pfeffer underscores a sobering, unpopular reality about leadership: "Faking it" is a key ingredient of leadership talent.[2] In fact, it is largely due to the preponderance of impression management and faking among leaders that the notion of authenticity may have caught fire in the first place: You need to be pretty insincere to pretend that you are being sincere! It goes without saying that if *not* being yourself is a career-enhancing strategy for employees and workers, it would be surprising to find a different strategy for interpersonal effectiveness in leaders, who are the employees or workers who climbed the organizational ladder, thus advancing their careers and becoming more successful. In fact, effective faking is even more important among leaders than employees. If you are unable (or unwilling) to adjust your behavior to meet social expectations, adhere to the dominant etiquette, take other people's perspectives into account, or make an effort to manage impressions so as to present yourself in a desirable way, then you won't just fail to be an effective leader, but will also probably fail to become a leader in the first place.[3]

As chapter 6 showed, inauthentic behaviors—such as modulating your emotional reactions, substituting uncomfortable truths with pleasant white lies, and telling people what they want to hear rather than what you think, especially when what you think is not what they want to hear (all of which must be done with social skills and emotional intelligence, and without violating basic ethical principles)—are critical to advancing your career. This includes attaining positions of leadership, which is a universal marker of success because it involves reaching the top of an organizational ladder or social hierarchy.[4]

In fact, once you become a leader, being able to master the art of effective inauthenticity is even more critical, not just for your own benefit, but for other people's as well. Alas, we are inundated with examples of leaders who neglect the need to edit their behaviors and instead decide to unleash their authentic self on others. Indeed, the often-quoted adage that "power corrupts, and absolute power corrupts absolutely" sheds light on the dangers of authenticity taken too far. When leaders feel powerful and entitled, they indulge in expressing their unfiltered and uncensored self at work, with little consideration for what others think of them, or they incrementally dismiss impression management as they gain power and become less accountable or responsible for their acts. Although we may celebrate such behaviors in antihero and antiestablishment figures that appear to "stick it to the man," in the real world they are simply examples of leaders who act without regard for others' feelings, behaving in unprofessional, toxic, and even destructive ways.[5] Among corporate executives, billionaire entrepreneurs, senior politicians, and heads of state (not to mention dictators), many leaders start as relatively benevolent and inspirational role models before deteriorating into parasitic creatures. Charismatic qualities and charming manipulation skills may mask their narcissistic tendencies at first, but once they accrue sufficient status and power to no longer care about managing their own reputation, their "authentic self" reveals their true dark side, which they no longer care to hide.[6]

Likewise, bosses who focus too much on "being themselves," perhaps encouraged by the popularity of the authenticity cult, will often create detrimental cultures, forcing their subordinates and direct reports to put up with their immature and childish behaviors. The characters David Brent and Michael Scott from *The Office* provide us with cathartic opportunities to laugh and relieve some of the pain of actually having put up with a very similar type of boss. Said boss could simply improve their performance significantly by editing their behavior, caring about how they impact others, and making an effort to manage their reputation. Of course, that would make for a very boring TV show or mockumentary if they did—"good bosses" or "nice bosses" would be far less funny and, sadly, less close to reality. If you have ever worked for someone who displays a lack of professionalism, including inappropriate jokes or casual behavior that make employees uncomfortable, you will understand firsthand how painful and dreadful it is to be on the receiving end of managerial or leadership authenticity. And because such bosses are also prone to ignore feedback from others, especially their own employees, the likelihood that they will improve is slim.

Among the many negative consequences created by leader or manager authenticity, we include inconsistent and unpredictable behaviors, which arise when a boss's actions fluctuate, where sometimes they adhere to prosocial and culturally acceptable norms, but more often they neglect them to show their true thoughts, feelings, and values in defiance of organizational citizenship. This leaves employees unsure about how to navigate interactions. Favoritism can also become an issue if a boss naturally leans toward certain employees based on personal preferences, thus creating perceptions of bias and an unfair culture. Why? Because if leaders follow their values and are true to their emotions and thoughts, they are likely to prefer some colleagues and workers over others, even when this represents and legitimizes their biases rather than provides a rational or data-driven appraisal of their team's performance.

Additionally, authenticity breeds overconfidence, since not caring about what others think of you, and acting according to your own drives, impulses, and thoughts without editing them can lead to bosses taking unnecessary risks without consulting the team, thus resulting in project failures or inefficiencies. Moreover, the dismissal of cultural sensitivity—since a boss who considers only their perspective may unintentionally offend employees from diverse backgrounds—is far more likely to occur when bosses decide they can just be themselves. And a disregard for others' views and needs leads to a toxic environment, reduced morale, and higher turnover, as employees feel unappreciated and unvalued—unless they are privileged or fortunate to be part of the "tribe," or the high-status ingroup.

In essence, most of the social, political, and economic problems that leaders cause are a direct result of their unwillingness or inability to hold back their authentic self, usually because they feel too powerful, immune, or entitled to care about the consequences of acting with too little consideration for what others need, and with too much consideration for their own interests. Consider some high-profile examples. Elon Musk confessed to being high on social media, threatened to take Tesla private, picked fights with heads of state, and ignited social unrest at home and abroad (not to mention the fact that he randomly accused honest and moral people of being pedophiles). Then there is Donald Trump's invitation for his supporters to storm the Capitol in reaction to his refusal to admit that he lost the presidential election; the constant attacks on the LGBT+ community by J. K. Rowling (or Dave Chappelle); or Kanye West's uninhibited antisemitic remarks. It is important to note that these are some of the most popular and successful role models of today's society, and their actions may often be interpreted as a validation of authenticity and "just being yourself" no matter what. But the causality underpinning this correlation goes in the other direction—because of the power, popularity, and status these figures enjoy, they are able to "just be themselves" and unleash their authenticity on others. In other words, authenticity is a perk for the privileged few, the elite, or the status quo who can afford to behave however they want and on whichever day they feel like, because their status and power confers entitlement and immunity. Sad, but true.

Whatever we think of these political, business, cultural, and artistic leaders, there is no question that they behave in rather more authentic ways than the average human—at times to their own peril (their decision, fine), but even more often without considering the pain and harm they inflict on others, not least when they incite violence in the name of freedom of speech and anti-censorship. In a way, the world's main leadership problems (which underpin most of the greatest problems in the world) don't happen because leaders fake it, but because they *stop* faking it, and suddenly feel that they have the right to just be themselves. Likewise, the best attempts to develop, coach, or improve leaders so they can be more effective in having a positive impact on others, would converge on one specific goal: to help them to *not* be themselves. In other words, the goal is to help them develop the necessary skills—and especially motivation—to censor, constrain, and control their authentic or real selves.

How Authenticity Backfires

Rather than focusing on being nice, ethical, and competent, and being perceived as trustworthy by others, especially followers, leaders often view authenticity as an end goal, as if it was a critical enabler of their success.[7] However, focusing too much on authenticity—in this case, adhering too closely to the "just be yourself" mantra—will foster a narcissistic mindset that is not conducive to leadership effectiveness. Instead, leaders would be better off if they focused on being other-oriented, so as to understand how other people think and feel in order to enable them to work together. In order to achieve this, they must display signs of integrity, conscientiousness, altruism, and prosocial intentions, which rarely happens when they stop caring about what others think of them. It's really quite simple: The more leaders focus on themselves, the less they'll focus on, or care about, others. To be sure, not all the leaders who decide to be themselves or unleash their authentic selves are narcissistic, and many don't have the typical features of a toxic or parasitic personality either. Still, there are usually trade-offs between the impulse to express one's uncensored, uninhibited self, and the basic demands of professionalism.

Consider the timely challenge modern leaders face today, regarding the pressure—or at least temptation—to express their unsolicited and genuine moral views on salient and current political, social, or cultural events. For example, expressing their political or ideological views to their direct reports, such as condemning a presidential candidate, may be an effective strategy to gain popularity or win brownie points with those who share the same political preferences, but it will also alienate and antagonize those who don't, not to mention increase polarization, tribalization, and group divisions in the team. Or a leader who decides it is wise to share their candid and unfiltered views on abortion, immigration, climate change, or the wars in Ukraine and the Middle East: While we may praise them for "standing up" for any of these causes—or indeed against them—you are far less likely to accept such a person as a boss if your views are at the other extreme of the spectrum.

Likewise, bosses may feel tempted to not just share aspects of their private life with their teams, as if it signaled vulnerability and openness, but to even ask their reports about their personal and private life—after all, an authentic relationship is born out of knowing ourselves and each other really well, and having no secrets . . . Or is it? Not really! Just as managers should stay away from employees' private lives, they should also respect employees' desire to ignore their bosses' personal issues. In fact, whether they are our boss or direct report, there is no need to connect with someone on an extraprofessional level in order to work well with that person.

Since people with leadership aspirations are already more likely to be overconfident, and to think more highly of themselves than they should, a pursuit of authentic leadership can be a recipe for disaster—like throwing gasoline on a fire.[8] Authenticity fuels narcissism in both aspiring and incumbent leaders, encouraging them to ignore others and inflate their egos no matter what. Note that even if narcissistic leaders lack the actual talents to match their grandiose self-presentation, their confidence and bravado are often genuine, to the point of accurately reflecting their megalomaniacal visions, fantasized talents, and delusions of grandeur. This grandiose egomania leaves little room for self-doubt and distorts reality, lubricating and enhancing their already inflated egos. Appropriately, academic research identifies the core narcissism traits as entitlement, grandiose exhibitionism, exploitativeness, and—ironically—*leadership*.[9]

Research suggests that it is shockingly common for narcissistic individuals to become powerful leaders, particularly when they are male, as men still benefit from extra privilege or credit compared to women, hence their higher propensity to believe they can just be themselves.[10] Perhaps this explains why it's not terribly difficult to think of famous leaders who behave in entitled, self-important, overconfident, and self-absorbed ways. Or why a humble politician, entrepreneur, or business executive is as improbable as an Argentine vegan (in Argentina, which has the highest beef-per-capita consumption in the world, veganism is even more improbable than humility, and a vegetarian is "someone who enjoys their steak with a salad").

When leadership becomes less about guiding a team or organization, or turning a group of people into a high-performing unit—a force that makes people better together—and more of a selfish and individual career destination, a personal accolade, or the ultimate status signal, then a disproportionately high number of narcissists will be attracted to it. Worse still, leaders' narcissism often combines with psychopathic tendencies, resulting in a toxic mix.[11] While narcissism fuels an obsession with fame and success, psychopathy adds an appetite for breaking the rules and taking advantage of others. Both traits converge in a crucial way: lack of empathy or interest in what others think or feel. Nobody takes the "don't worry about what other people think," and especially *"feel,"* rule more seriously than psychopaths do.

It gets worse. Narcissistic and psychopathic leaders are often charismatic, which will make them far more destructive.[12] Charisma per se is neither good nor bad; it's an amplifier. So, when you have competent and ethical leaders, you want them to be as charismatic as possible, so they can maximize their positive impact and influence on others. But, when leaders are incompetent or unethical (or worse, both), their charisma only amplifies their harmful impact. In such cases, your best hope is that they have the charisma of a parking lot so their ability to influence others is minimal.

It is also noteworthy that charisma alone doesn't necessarily make leaders seem authentic, let alone effective. It's the actual alignment between the leader's and the group's values and needs that gives leaders legitimacy, and boosts their reputation for being genuine, effective, and authentic. As Alice Eagly, a renowned leadership scholar, notes: "Much more is required of leaders than transparently conveying and acting on their values. Achieving authenticity requires that followers accord leaders the legitimacy to promote a set of values on behalf of a community. Only under such conditions can leaders elicit the personal and social identification of followers that can enhance the success of a group, organization, or society."[13] Crucially, Eagly points out, it is useless for leaders to be true to their values, or to even communicate with them transparently, unless these values are shared by their followers and subordinates. So, we tend to seek leaders who channel our values, or express them in more practical, team-oriented ways.

What people want in a leader is someone who can give them a sense of direction, hope, and the vision of a better future. This requires articulating and conveying a picture that is compelling and keeping people believing in it. Fundamentally, in order to turn this vision into reality, leaders must be able to coordinate human activity, turn a group of people into a winning team (whether this team is a corporate business unit, an effective organization, or indeed a nation or society at large). The notion that any of this can happen—if leaders decide to somehow just be themselves, are true to their inner feelings or values, or stop worrying about what others think of them—is absurd, to put it mildly.

Sadly, the notion that authenticity is a pivotal ingredient of leadership has become a near-ubiquitous misconception, which explains the prevalent gap between the leaders we need and those we actually get. Consider a recent poll by Edelman's global trust barometer, which shows that almost 70 percent of the general public has no trust or confidence whatsoever in either business or political leaders (up from 57 percent in 2021); or that global employee engagement surveys consistently report that only three out of ten workers are enthusiastic or satisfied with their jobs; and that the number one reason for disliking—or even quitting—a job has to do with direct line managers.[14] As the saying goes, "People join companies but quit their bosses."[15] Moreover, stress and burnout, which is primarily caused by incompetent or toxic management, can be expected to impact three in four workers at some point of their careers.[16] Despite the prevalent distrust and dislike people have of AI, the World Economic Forum reports that over 80 percent of workers believe a robot would be better than a human boss.[17]

Clearly, then, when it comes to leadership, we have a big opportunity to improve the current state of affairs, not just for leaders but for everyone else. There is an opportunity to distinguish between style and substance, and between what's good for the leader and what's good for everyone else. On the former the issue is intuitive: Authenticity, just like confidence and charisma, is about style, rather than substance. We shouldn't care so much about whether leaders *really mean* what they say and do "deep down," so long as what they do is good for us, in the sense of making us work and achieve better results—together. On the latter, the road to progress is also pretty clear. Amid recurrent calls to incentivize workers to "just be themselves" and act in more authentic or true ways, it seems that a better approach to improving the state of affairs in the world would be to persuade those in charge—particularly when they lack leadership talent—to *not* be themselves, and to develop the ability to self-edit, self-censor, and transition from selfish and rude entitlement to altruistic and empathetic concern for others. Needless to say, if the choice is between a leader who is authentic but incompetent, and one who has worked hard to mitigate and inhibit their flaws so as to positively impact those they lead, it's a no-brainer.

Indeed, our choice is clear: We can either continue to see leadership as a personal privilege, which, alas, includes giving leaders license to "just be themselves," or we can start focusing on what it means to have certain people in charge of and responsible for others, controlling resources, and being a driving force of other people's performance, achievements, and well-being.

The Power of Going Against Your Nature

Even if you are a successful leader, your potential will depend on your ability to change, grow, and develop a new and different behavioral repertoire than the one that helped you succeed in the past. "What got you here won't get you there" is uniquely true among popular management clichés, in the sense that career advancement and personal development both demand adapting to a new range of challenges, and solving a new, often harder, set of problems.

Aside from the negative impact authenticity has on a leader's performance, the temptation to just be yourself will also inhibit your potential to improve and upgrade your leadership competence and talents. Indeed, no matter how good or bad leaders are, it's imperative that they continue to get better—a leader is always a work in progress, and a leader who thinks or feels they are a finished product is basically finished. So, sticking to your authentic self is extremely limiting in terms of preventing you from fulfilling or maximizing your potential. If you want to grow as a leader, you need to be open to new experiences, and the only way to learn from those experiences is to go outside your comfort zone, which means *not* acting in your same old natural or authentic ways, but rather experimenting with new behaviors and challenges. This calls for novel experiences, and the capacity to *not* be constrained by your current or past self. In other words, why limit yourself to who you are if you could actually broaden, enrich, or diversify yourself by acquiring new habits and strengths, and by expanding your adaptive toolkit through developing dispositions and responses that go beyond your natural inclinations, and even include the ability to react in ways that run counter to your personality. Your future self may contain your present and past self but it is hopefully more than just that.

Even feeling like a fake can be indicative of the fact that you are growing as a leader, for it signals your incursion into new behavioral terrains, unnatural actions, and beyond your habitual repertoire of thoughts, feelings, and behaviors—a notion brilliantly articulated by my dear friend and London Business School professor Herminia Ibarra, who pioneered a clear pathway for breaking the authenticity trap by broadening your current self with your future and possible selves.[18] As she astutely points out, we would be better off redefining authenticity to include the *potential* behaviors and actions that are possible, even (and perhaps especially) if they are not emblematic or archetypical of your past or present self. In that sense, the capacity to renew yourself and your identity—and become a more complex, rather than a more exaggerated, version of yourself—is what leaders ought to cultivate and develop. This requires not following tried-and-tested paths, or being true to your natural self, but rather going outside your comfort zone instead. It is more about broadening your self, than being true to your natural self. Partly, you will achieve this if you are open to exploring other people's values, rather than imposing your values on others, as well as doing things you would normally refrain from doing. There is always a first time, and some first unusual or unexpected experiences will end up becoming ingrained in new habits, thus contributing to your evolution and providing a critical pathway for the evolution of leadership, based on higher coachability levels.[19]

People love strength-based career advice and coaching, because it is always easier to do what you are already good at, but the "play to your strength" mantra is simply another form of "just be yourself" or "do what feels natural." Judged in subjective terms, it may no doubt be comforting to do what you enjoy doing and what comes easy to you. However, this doesn't guarantee that others are impressed by that skill, that the skill is in demand, or that you will be able to apply it in a wide range of settings.[20] Moreover, it almost certainly guarantees that you will not focus on developing new skills or strengths, and even virtues and sought-after skills become weaknesses when overdone or taken to the extreme. As leadership expert and scholar Rob Kaiser has demonstrated in a compelling line of research assessing leadership talent and effectiveness, the greatest leaders are actually *versatile*, in the sense that they manage to learn how to flex into the opposite direction that they are naturally predisposed to going.[21] In that sense, your talent as a leader is a function of the multitude of adaptations, tendencies, and behavioral skills you have in your toolkit, in your repertoire: the more complex, diverse, and unpredictable you are, the wider the range of challenges you will be able to effectively address as a leader.

If you are always performing well without stretching yourself, you are probably not developing. If you are always playing to your strengths, you are probably not getting stronger. If you are cruising and delivering results on autopilot, you are at risk of stagnating and not maximizing or unlocking your full potential, let alone evolving.

The evolution of you, if you are a leader, centers very much around your ability to go against your natural tendencies and impulses, to defy your default authentic behaviors and reactions to events and stimuli, or to learn new skills. It's like the person who goes to the gym, but always exercises the same muscles—they will be disproportionately shaped, imbalanced, and strong at only one or two things.

This counterintuitive philosophy of improving leadership potential and performance by reducing, rather than augmenting, authenticity in leaders can also be applied to coaching, which is the process of assisting leaders in their personal and professional development aspirations in order to help them upgrade their potential and performance. My own approach to coaching senior leaders and executives involves poking and poking until a weakness is revealed—an underutilized or dormant muscle that risks atrophy unless it is used or developed. This could be political skills, empathy, self-control, humility, self-criticism, or self-awareness. All coaching should include an assessment of what may actually be wrong, or at least needs fixing or improving, with a leader's authentic self—in the sense that the person they evoke or display in their typical work interactions with others needs a little tweaking or retooling. This is where self-awareness is critical: It's the journey of helping leaders understand their reputation in order to motivate them to close the gap between how they are seen by others and how they would like to be seen. Leaders who engage in formal coaching programs tend to improve their behaviors and performance by acting on their weaknesses—or if you prefer the HR euphemism for weaknesses, then "opportunities"— and displaying the necessary behaviors to influence how other people see them.[22] All leadership potential, then, will include the ability to go against your nature, and to become a less exaggerated version of yourself. Executive and leadership coaching can be extremely impactful in enabling this in leaders, even in a short time frame. Research shows that even a few weeks of coaching can help people build better interpersonal and intrapersonal adaptations, keep counterproductive emotions in check, and develop new, effective adaptations.[23]

Making others better

It is not sufficient for a leader to go against their own nature; they must also help others do the same. Great leaders serve as catalysts for the development and improvement of those around them. This means not only recognizing and hiring for potential, but actively nurturing and cultivating it as well—which includes empowering and guiding people in their journey of becoming more than who they already are, and amplifying, augmenting, enriching, and diversifying their professional self.

A great leader, like a great sports coach or fitness instructor, helps others build and develop beyond their capabilities and strengths. This means encouraging others to go beyond their authentic self, as well as helping others to identify with *new* elements of their selves, so they can revise and redefine their personal identity to absorb and incorporate their expanded and refreshed reputation. To achieve this, leaders must largely quench individuals' self-righteous displays of authenticity to make them more other-oriented—tolerant of the values and needs of others—so they can set aside their selfish interests to be part of a stronger, more capable unit. This is how leaders turn a group of B players into an A team. By suppressing people's narcissistic needs and convincing them that if they care less about themselves and more about the group, they can be part of something bigger than themselves, and achieve something they would not have been able to achieve alone. Conversely, when leaders allow for selfish, egotistical, narcissistic, and individualistic efforts to prevail, even A players will become a B or C team.

We're part of the problem, too

While it's easy to place the blame for poor leadership squarely on the shoulders of, well, bad leaders, it's important to recognize another part of the problem: their followers. And by followers, I mean all of us—for even leaders are still followers.

As the world grows in complexity and uncertainty, we crave meaning and sensemaking, which makes it harder for leaders to emerge when they have the humility and self-critical awareness to acknowledge that things are complex, life is uncertain, and doubt is more warranted than conviction. In contrast, those leaders who elicit a false sense of security (of having control over things), who promise simple solutions, and who vow to change the world rather than their followers, feed into the self-centered aspirations of people's desire to "just be themselves," unleashing followers' biases and selling the rhetoric that everything is *the other's* fault.

Some of us would prefer a leader who tells us we're great. This kind of affirmation validates our sense of self and identity, but it doesn't motivate us or anyone else to change or grow. There are also only short-term benefits to following someone because they provide us with a much rosier picture of reality, a boost to our self-esteem, or a compelling vision of the world that relies primarily on distorting facts in a self-serving way, to the point that we end up delusional and trapped in an imaginative, egotistical alternate reality; alas, actual reality doesn't just go away because we stop thinking about it.

. . .

In conclusion, the romanticized notion of leader authenticity often obscures a deeper, more nuanced truth: Great leaders are not those who merely stay true to their unfiltered selves, but rather those who adapt, grow, and transcend their natural inclinations for the sake of others. Authenticity, when unchecked, can lead to narcissism, entitlement, and even harm. Instead, the hallmark of effective leadership lies in the willingness to step outside one's comfort zone, cultivate self-awareness, and embrace behaviors that prioritize collective success over individual self-expression. Leadership is not about personal validation or self-righteous displays, but about inspiring, nurturing, and uniting others to achieve shared goals. It is also not about what or how leaders feel, but rather how they impact others. By focusing less on being authentic and more on being effective, leaders can transform not only themselves, but also the teams, organizations, and societies they serve. Furthermore, it is not sufficient for leaders to enable *others* to express their authentic self, though this notion sounds appealing for sure. Rather, it is helping others bring, discover, or create the best version of themselves, and managing the tensions between expressing their authentic and professional identity in the interest of their colleagues, team, and organization, that constitute the bastion of leadership talent. In short, the best leaders are not there to enable people to just be themselves, or feel good about their self, but rather to help them become part of a highly functioning unit, a winning team, so they can contribute something valuable to the wider world of organizations, institutions, societies, and progress; something that is bigger and better than their own individual and selfish needs.

8

Diversity and Inclusion

An important milestone in the history of diversity and inclusion (D&I)* is the recent realization that organizational diversity—defined as the degree of demographic or psychological heterogeneity in a workforce—is not sufficient to either reduce counterproductive

*For the sake of simplicity, I will focus on *diversity* and *inclusion* (D&I), though it is important to acknowledge that some of the points made also apply to *equity* and *belonging*, which are typically bundled together under the D&I acronym. Diversity refers to the presence of differences within a given setting, encompassing various dimensions (including race, ethnicity, gender, age, sexual orientation, disability, and socioeconomic status). The goal of diversity initiatives is not merely to populate an organization with a wide array of individuals, but to harness these differences in a way that enriches the organizational culture and outputs as well. Equity involves ensuring fair treatment, equality of opportunity, and advancement for all individuals, while striving to identify and eliminate barriers that have prevented the full participation of some groups. This requires understanding the root causes of outcome disparities within the organization and in society at large. Inclusion is the practice of creating environments in which any individual or group feel welcomed, respected, supported, and valued. Belonging refers to the experience of being part of a community or organization where one is valued, and where one's contributions are appreciated. It goes beyond simple inclusion to foster a sense of integral importance to the group's success.

or unfair obstacles to individuals who don't belong to a normative in-group, or to ignite an organization's potential for creativity and inno-vation. In fact, unless you first create an inclusive culture, in which outgroup individuals are as able to thrive as ingroup individuals, di-versity will backfire.[1] This is no different from governments deciding to open its borders to more migrants, without tackling the prejudiced and discriminatory forces that impede their progress—which will re-sult in even more prejudice.

It is within this context that many organizations have decided to em-phasize authenticity as a strategic imperative to advance their D&I interventions. In particular, commands, requests, or, at minimum, invi-tations to "be yourself" are disproportionately directed at outgroup individuals, which unintentionally reinforces the idea that authenticity is a privilege for the ingroup. For example, LGBT+ employees are often encouraged to share their sexual orientation or gender identification; cultural minorities (whether by race, ethnicity, nationality, or social class) are told there is no need to conform to the dominant etiquette or behavioral habits of the ingroup, when it comes to either adjusting their dress code, accents, or self-presentational style; and of course, women (not so much a statistical minority as the disadvantaged sex) are invited to provide the "feminine touch" (i.e., embracing their archetypical or traditional femininity) by bringing empathy and prosocial traits to the workplace, and to ensure that their "feminine thinking" or perspective, not to mention feeling, is always added to the mix.

Indeed, many organizations went as far as offering authenticity as an employment benefit, a sort of company perk that allegedly re-moves the social pressures to conform or self-edit. For example, Salesforce, LinkedIn, Google, and Microsoft focus on creating inclu-sive environments where employees can be authentic, with an em-phasis on diversity, inclusion, and psychological safety. Airbnb and Ben & Jerry's promote belonging and individuality, aligning their internal culture with their external social justice missions, while Zappos fosters a fun, quirky atmosphere that values personal expression. These companies use authenticity as a key marketing tool to attract diverse talent, highlighting that employees can thrive by being true to themselves, which also enhances engagement and retention.

Some employees see this "right" as congruent with their efforts to access jobs that are a strong fit for their own personal beliefs, dispositions, and preferences. After all, if a company is able to attract a diverse range of people, it must also enable them to act as the individuals they are, and invite them to express their psychological uniqueness, values, and personalities, rather than force them to conform to some ingroup norms.[2]

Proponents of D&I initiatives argue that these programs are not only compatible with authenticity, but an essential foundation for its realization in professional settings.[3] They even suggest that by creating an environment where diverse identities and perspectives are actively valued and included, D&I interventions lay the groundwork for authentic self-expression, thus harnessing creativity and innovation in organizations from the bottom up.

In such environments, workers are less likely to feel the need to conceal or alter aspects of their identity in order to fit in, as the diversity of experiences and backgrounds is not only accepted, but also celebrated and recognized as a strength. While all this may be well-intended, it is actually quite problematic, to say the least . . .

Wrong Assumptions

The first problem with D&I initiatives is that they assume that outgroup individuals are actually interested in standing out, being different, and sharing their private thoughts, attitudes, and views with others, especially when they conflict with the ingroup's views. Needless to say, since authenticity is more likely to drive incompetence than competence in the ingroup, there's a flawed logic to assuming that the outgroup should somehow attempt to emulate this. As Oliver Burkeman noted, "The solution to a world run by many incompetent fools is not to make the rest of the world incompetent, too."[4]

Second, there is usually a cost to acting authentically or being yourself when you are not part of the ingroup. So, while a growing number of D&I interventions include authenticity as a strategic imperative, thus prompting minority, low status, and outgroup candidates to just be themselves and bring their whole self to work (which is obviously less of a perk if it feels like an imposition or obligation that takes away the right to *not* be yourself), authenticity is far more natural as a behavioral approach if people belong to the ingroup, have high status, or represent the status quo. For example, it should not surprise anyone that leaders find it significantly easier to be authentic if they are male rather than female, white rather than Black, rich rather than poor, and so on. The fact of the matter is that only those who enjoy a certain level of status, privilege, or power are truly allowed to be themselves, and it doesn't generally end up very well. In contrast, those who are not part of the ingroup may well be invited to be themselves, but they are likely to be punished if they actually comply with such commands or accept such invitations.

It's understandable that authenticity emerges as a privilege of those who already acquired status and success. As noted in the previous chapter, the phrase "power corrupts and absolute power corrupts absolutely" explains the simple fact that the more successful you are, the more you can afford to be yourself, by ignoring what people think of you.[5] Or demanding that they like the version of you that you were forced to suppress when you were not yet successful, but in the process of accumulating power . . .

This also explains why people differ (sadly, a priori) in their freedom to be themselves. Some tailwinds—race, social class, gender, and even the luck needed to be born in the right place at the right time and to the right people—enable people to unleash their impulsive, spontaneous, and uninhibited selves without too much consideration of others, and to the detriment of everybody else. They were born into privilege, enjoyed confidence-boosting, and opportunity-enhancing (aka rich) parents, and lived a relatively failure-free life (or at least their failures were cheap and inconsequential). On the downside, this could make them unjustifiably pleased with themselves, and unaware of their limitations. If you grow up thinking you are the hero in your parents' minds, sooner or later you will have a reality check. At the same time, it is quite possible that your delusions or reality distortions will end up becoming self-fulfilling, and thus persuade others that you are as great as you think you are, not least when they already admire you for your privileges—charisma and a winning personality are far more likely to be attributed to people who come from the ingroup rather than the outgroup.

To be sure, people can be quite proud of their headwinds or disadvantages, which usually inhibit their ability to assert or impose their authentic self on others, not least because it enables them to showcase their resilience, toughness, and grit. In the famous *Monty Python* sketch known as "The Four Yorkshiremen," four well-dressed men sit together, reminiscing about their ostensibly impoverished childhoods in Yorkshire. As they sip wine in a luxurious setting, their tales of hardship grow increasingly outlandish and competitive. The sketch humorously satirizes the tendency to romanticize the tough past and engage in one-upmanship over who had the most difficult upbringing. Each man claims his family was poorer than the others, recounting absurdly exaggerated stories of living in holes in the ground, waking up before they went to bed, and working unimaginable hours for a pittance. The sketch then famously escalates as each story becomes more ludicrous, involving eating gravel for dinner and being thrashed to sleep by their fathers. Despite the apparent misery of their tales, the men speak with a sense of nostalgic pride, as if their extreme poverty was a badge of honor, resulting from their ability to adapt and adjust to adverse circumstances—rather than the privilege to just be themselves.

The irony is hard to miss: Even those who enjoyed a privileged upbringing will attempt to claim hardship, if only because it reflects more meritocratically on their achievements—the less luck or nepotism played a role, the more we can attribute their success to talent or effort. Perhaps this explains why in an age that often glorifies, if not weaponizes, D&I, ingroup individuals will often pretend to be part of the outgroup, which, in a way, signals an attempt to not be themselves!

Regardless of what organizations tell them about authenticity, employees' decisions to behave in more or less constrained ways will depend more on their perception of the company culture, and their experience of what is rewarded or sanctioned—trust, unsurprisingly, being always of the essence. For instance, research indicates that low status individuals tend to act more openly and express their personal selves more often when they actually trust others to welcome this, or when they perceive an environment that welcomes their authentic selves. Indeed, when outgroup or low status individuals experience lower levels of discrimination, they are more likely to express personal or private aspects of their identify at work, which in turn produces higher levels of person-organization fit and job satisfaction.[6] Clearly, simply telling people to bring their whole selves to work and be themselves is not enough. Claims must be backed up by actions, companies must put their money where their mouth is, and employees must actually feel safe to act without concern of punishment. By definition, if you have to tell them that they can be themselves, they probably don't feel that this is true.

Another important data point comes from research on self-monitoring, the main psychological measure to account for someone's propensity to pay attention to how others see them, and to adjust their behavior to make a positive impression on them (and to avoid making a negative one). In general, self-monitoring is positively associated with career success, including performance ratings: More often than not, your boss will appreciate if you make an effort to *not* be yourself (a feeling that is generally mutual). That said, the propensity to engage in self-monitoring is especially true for outgroup rather than ingroup employees. For example, while we ask women to be themselves, it is clear that they must go to even greater lengths than men to present their best professional self, and modify their behavior to adhere to cultural norms, than men do. The particular challenge they face is that they are forced to conform to a greater degree than men, but at the same time are also punished more when their behavior seems unnatural or inauthentic. Meanwhile, men generally enjoy greater license to just be themselves, but they still advance their careers through self-monitoring and impression management.[7] So, women are doomed whether they fake it or not, and men are fine whether they fake it or not.

Even when the impact of self-monitoring in performance ratings is small, it can have a big consequence for gender representation in leadership. As a meta-analysis in this area reports, you only need as little as 1 percent of anti-women bias in performance appraisal to end up with 15 percent fewer women in leadership roles.[8] In other words, even tiny differences in performance ratings of men and women can cause substantial differences in the relative progress of men and women in organizations, irrespective of their actual leadership potential or talent. The implications are rather obvious: If your gender D&I intervention consists of telling women to refrain from self-monitoring, to just be themselves, to express what they feel, and to not worry about what others think of them, they will face pretty adverse repercussions—for these privileges are generally more likely to be conferred to men. Same goes for other outgroup employees—trying to opt into any authenticity perks will harm their career prospects more than if they were part of the ingroup.

Gender is the most universal demographic category in D&I interventions. Anywhere in the world, women, more so than men, face biased adverse impacts, glass ceilings, prejudice, and discrimination, despite not only representing a statistical majority in the world, but also outnumbering and outperforming men at universities, and displaying more of the bright-side qualities that make people better leaders, and fewer of the dark-side ones. So, which gender research revelations apply to other demographic or diversity groups? Substitute gender with sexual orientation, ethnicity, social class, nationality, age (unless the job is president of the United States), or your favorite category of neurodiversity, and the same rule applies: The higher your status, the closer you are to the status quo, the more privilege you enjoy, and the more we tolerate your authentic behaviors. Conversely, the lower rank or status you have, the more you must comply and conform to the norms and rules set by the elite or the status quo.

How odd, then, that authenticity is sold as a mainstream D&I intervention and as a kind of perk offered to outgroup workers, when these individuals have additional pressure to self-monitor, conform, and adjust their behavior to fit in with the norm.

The Say-Do Gap

Needless to say, a common problem with D&I interventions is the gap between what companies say and actually do, which in itself questions the authenticity of such interventions.[9] Particularly in leaders, the "say-do" gap will determine not only whether they are perceived by others as authentic, but also ethical. Since words are cheap, and everybody seems to know what to say, people are increasingly skeptical when they hear almost every leader give media-savvy D&I promises and express strong levels of commitment to prosocial causes, but without the actions to back it up. In fact, describing one's culture as diverse and inclusive—and telling people that everyone is welcome to bring their whole self to work, to just be themselves, and that they will be loved for expressing their authentic self and true values—forms part of this common virtue signaling. Sure, there are exceptions, but in the vast majority of cases, these promises reflect words rather than facts.

Hypocritical contradictions frequently underpin gender diversity interventions, which simultaneously nudge and celebrate women for just being themselves, while persistently trying to "fix them," make them more like men, and actually mold them into a model of leadership that rarely includes effectiveness, altruism, empathy, and the qualities that make leaders better (and that make women, in general, better leaders than men). For instance, women are told that they should speak in meetings even if they have nothing to say; they should apply for jobs even when they only meet one or two of the ten criteria required to be qualified; and they should overcome their imposter syndrome, rid themselves of self-doubt, and just believe in themselves, be confident, and lean in.

In essence, this advice is based on the premise that the kind of leaders we often see at the top of organizations—privileged, narcissistic men—are some kind of a golden role model or ideal profile, which implies they were put there for meritocratic reasons. Hence, if only women could learn to behave like them in a more self-centered, overconfident, and entitled way, they too would be able to get to the top!

Aside from the obvious contradiction between this and any advice preaching authenticity, the most detrimental issue at stake here is that outdoing narcissistic males in terms of masculinity may not even advance women's careers—a double bind causes social expectations to resist non-feminine behaviors in women, including coming across as pathologically ambitious. And if and when women advance through such means, everybody suffers, including the people who need to work for such women, and the other women who are actually equipped with the foundational ingredients that predict strong leadership potential. Because for every woman that fails, negative stereotypes and prejudices against all women as leaders are cemented, fueled, and confirmed.

We aren't pre-wired for diversity

For the largest portion of our human evolution, our lives were not optimized for D&I, but rather for quashing our social curiosity and open-mindedness, and refraining from unnecessary displays of non-pragmatic novelty-seeking and experimentation, at least when it came to learning about other humans.

Our hunter-gatherer ancestors, who lived and worked with the same small group of largely related people, and wandered nomadically from one place to another in the search of food, were just not that interested in being inclusive.[10] If someone from a particular group or clan wished to display their open-minded curiosity in order to wander around in search of a rival clan, just for the sake of getting to know people who were different (either because they were bored hanging out with the same people all their lives, or perhaps because they wanted to put in practice what they learned in their unconscious bias training seminars), they would have been beaten, killed, or eaten (or any combination of those). Failing that, their best prospect would have been to return to their clan with a whole new range of parasites and infections that would have weakened or wiped out their own people. Indeed, evolutionary psychology suggests that one of the best explanations for the fact that warmer cultures tend to be less curious or open to new experiences, is that the risk of parasitic infection is much higher there.[11]

It is unreasonable to expect anyone to like everyone else, especially if everyone else is not making an effort to *not* be themselves, fit in, or focus on the collective harmony. Our instinct, which is the operating system we inherited from our evolutionary ancestors, pretty much tells us to distrust or dislike those who are different from us. This instinct has done a pretty good job protecting us: We are all the descendants of people who succeeded at not being killed or eaten by others, largely because they distrusted anyone outside their clan or kin group. In this context, we need to realistically evaluate the modern attempts to get people to not only respect or tolerate those who are different from them, but also embrace and celebrate them; and the only conclusion to this assessment is that such attempts are simply unrealistic, because they expect us to unlearn thousands of years of evolution and erase mental shortcuts that always create a bias for those who seem more related or similar to ourselves.

That is not to say that we cannot improve: Culture has the ability to override, or at least subsume, our biological or evolutionary heritage. We are no longer hunter-gatherers, and modern methods of collaboration, coupled with a moral imperative and a business case, mean that people can be incentivized to not just work with strangers, but also trust those who seem markedly different from themselves. But do not be fooled: All of this requires effort, practice, external incentives (including rewards, sanctions, and extrinsic motives), and a willingness to not act according to our natural instincts or principles. Although organizations may see authenticity as compatible with inclusion, authenticity emphasizes individuality, whereas inclusion focuses on collective harmony and equity. This applies at the national culture level as well: If you migrate from Saudi Arabia to Sweden, you will need to adjust your authentic behaviors and style in an effort to fit in, integrate, and be accepted—same goes for migrating from Sweden to Saudi Arabia. This means paying special attention to what you say and do, and how that may impact others.

Even if you happen to work somewhere that adheres to the notion that "you can say what you like, but without hurting others"—which seems to wisely dilute radical authenticity or freedom of expression through the filter of empathy, kindness, and consideration—the rule is less robust than it may sound, since anything you say (or don't say) may end up hurting others. Granted, you may be concerned about not upsetting others and still upset them accidentally, inadvertently, or perhaps due to lack of cultural sensitivity or an excess of sensitivity in others, but those who don't focus on this *at all* will generally end up being far more frequent offenders. For instance, we can all accidentally make a seemingly inoffensive and innocent joke—at least according to our own standards or beliefs—that ends up upsetting others, but it is also possible to refrain from making jokes in the first place, precisely because of the risks that they may hurt someone. There is no room for freedom of speech unless you don't care about the prospect of upsetting or hurting others, and even if you prefer to avoid freedom of speech, that's no guarantee that you will not hurt others.

Likewise, microaggressions—which represent mostly unintentional displays of prejudice toward others, often masked behind the subtleties of idiomatic choices—may still be offensive and harmful. Microaggressions highlight the fact that even *not* expressing our immediate or spontaneous thoughts to others does not guarantee that we won't hurt them.[12] For example, when someone tells an outgroup, unconventional, diverse, or low-status individual that they must be good at something because of their group membership (e.g., Asians and science, women at being kind, and Latinos and dancing), the emitter of these messages may intend to give a compliment, but in fact unconsciously confirms racial stereotypes (which, albeit positive, may also imply deficits in other, group-incongruent skill areas). Here, the recipient of these messages would benefit from paying attention to the hidden meaning, for it would reveal the prejudiced biases of the sender, irrespective of whether their reaction is to be upset, confront, pretend to ignore, or even politely accept the compliments. Conversely, ignoring or being unaware of the senders' bias would not just limit their ability to understand the senders' character and values, but also miss an opportunity to shape their own reputation as seen by the sender. In order to change the rules of the game, you must first become aware of the rules, and then play within them; so if you want to persuade others to see you in a positive way, or think of you in a specific way, you must first become aware of what they think of you (i.e., what is the starting point or baseline for your reputation).

Compared to overt aggressions, not to mention macroaggressions, microaggressions are a First World problem.[13] Not a trivial one, of course, and some would argue harder to confront or tackle because they are invisible—similar to people who are passive aggressive and backstab you even while smiling and agreeing with you in public, and are thus much harder to expose and combat (compared to those who fight openly and share their views). This explains why the emotionally intelligent approach to disliking your colleagues is far more strategic and effective than the honest, authentic, and candid approach to confrontation.

By the same token, being overly concerned with what others think will lead to absolute silence and inaction. As Dostoyevsky famously lamented in a rant that would fit in perfectly with the current anti-woke movement: "Tolerance will reach such a level that intelligent people will be banned from thinking so as not to offend the imbeciles."

Still, the fact of the matter is that people differ significantly in their tendency to care about what others think of them, and those who care more will go the greater lengths to minimize the prospects of upsetting others, which usually impacts whether they actually succeed in doing so.

To be sure, it is generally better to discourage certain people from expressing their true values and attitudes if you want to protect out-group candidates from anti-D&I behaviors, like prejudiced discrimination, bullying, harassment, and antisocial conduct.[14] For example, if people are sexist, racist, ageist, anti-Semitic, or homophobic, you may not want them to bring their whole self to work, which would include expressing their authentic views on these matters. Indeed, would you rather know how these people are, particularly if you are on the receiving end of these antisocial prejudices, or would you prefer to have them pretend they are none of these things, to the point that you would never even suspect them of being prejudiced? While it is perhaps tempting to assume that it is always best to know who others truly are—including the worst aspect of their character and identity—no group, collective, or society can function with a minimum of harmony unless everybody makes an effort to hide their behavioral and mental dirt.

You can safely apply the same rule to yourself. Even if you don't identify with any of these prejudices, you can make an effort to be civil and cordial to others, and to hide other prejudiced beliefs (we all have them), as opposed to having them spill over to your actions and behaviors. It is noteworthy that people have a strong tendency to share their prejudices and antisocial beliefs with others, especially those they perceive as like-minded, in order to bond with them: By establishing common ground, reaffirming their mutual dislike, including hatred, of certain groups, classes, and individuals, they actually recycle their spite into a sort of prosocial lubricant. However, bonding with some colleagues over your shared prejudices is a toxic strategy for maintaining a positive reputation at work, not dissimilar to being a schoolyard bully, aside from being a pathetic way of feeling good about yourself by bringing other people down. You may not be responsible for your first, instinctive thought; but you are responsible for your second thought, and especially your behaviors. Clearly, trying to monitor, police, or control people's thoughts is very difficult, not to mention ethically questionable and often useless in preventing bad behaviors. This is why the best we can hope is to censor and inhibit problematic actions. Think what you like about anyone and anything, but be sensitive to others when you decide to act or share your thoughts with them.

Fortunately, decades of research show that the relationship between attitudes and behaviors is complex and nuanced, suggesting that humans are perfectly capable of acting in ways contrary to their beliefs, or of holding beliefs that do not match their habitual behaviors.[15] This doesn't make us a fraudulent species, it just makes us superior to a firefly or a fish. We may expect others to express their beliefs with sincerity, but our preference is that they act in a civilized and prosocial way, ideally while still seeming genuine. Forcing people to embrace and celebrate those who act, feel, and think in diametric opposition to themselves is unrealistic. However, it is also not necessary: For many centuries, even the average human with zero D&I training has been able to pretend to like their colleagues, bosses, and neighbors, while venting and b-tching about them as soon as they find themselves in the privacy of their homes, where they can reunite with their own whole self!

In essence, if you want to create a tolerant environment in which people feel free to speak up and feel free to express themselves without constraints or censorship, you need to first promote civility and tolerance. Because we cannot expect people to naturally self-regulate or self-edit, we must create environments where it is clear that proso-cial behaviors are rewarded and antisocial behaviors are sanctioned. The clearer these cultural norms and terms for social interaction are, the easier it will be for everybody to be conscious of their own behav-iors and actions—to the point of carefully modulating oneself, self-censoring, and picking the right course of action with delicate tact—in order to avoid inadvertently (or deliberately) harming others. And with time, all this will come so naturally that hardly any effort will be required to do it.

We should remember that humans are inherently biased, in the sense that we are permanently taking mental shortcuts in order to translate the ambiguous information of our environment into (seem-ingly) meaningful thoughts, ideas, and convictions. Our devotion to meaning and sense-making, even in the absence of meaning, propels us to fabricate it and make it up. We are meaning-making machines, with minimal need for actual facts or objective data—data tells, but stories sell, and our ability to fill in the gaps to create a seemingly ra-tional and plausible story in the absence of any logic underpins not just conspiracy theories, but also our own sense of identity. We write the script or story of who we are so as to give meaning to everything we do. In doing so, our ultimate goal is not so much to understand reality as it is, but to paint a picture of the world and ourselves that validates our positive self-views. Rather than blaming social media and big tech for the preponderance of fake news and the filter bubble, it would be useful to understand that these technological inventions are simply catering to our universal preference for hearing what we want to hear, and seeing what we want to see. Today it's AI, X, and tribalized mainstream media, but for centuries we had village gossip, magical beliefs, and Greek Gods—they all share a common purpose, namely to provide us with stories and narratives that become the scaffolding for our beliefs, and they lead us to make cushy interpretations of the world, allowing us to experience a false sense of certainty and security by making things seem coherent and predictable. Self-deception, the unconscious attempt to protect our self-concept by distorting reality in our favor, is the mother of all biases, because most biases are self-serving and self-enhancing.

This is not to say that we should resign ourselves to giving up on rationality, or give up hopes of an accurate understanding of the world. Still, we must be realistic about our ability to achieve this, and understand the potential downsides of doing so: We would not be able to function in everyday life if we had to stop to "think slow" about our preferences, decisions, and other people, every time we interact with them. Life happens fast and requires us to react instinctively and take most things for granted. For example, you just have to assume that the restaurant waiter isn't trying to poison you, that the taxi driver is sober, and that the doctor is interested in improving your health (to be sure, there's no shortage of stories highlighting the negative consequences of such assumptions being wrong, but they represent an exception rather than the norm). We tend to focus on the "ugly" type of biases—social biases, such as stereotypes and prejudices, that nurture interpersonal conflict and inequality—but most of the decisions we make on a regular basis are made in default or autopilot mode, and our capacity (and willingness) to become aware of these biases is indeed very limited. As the Nobel Prize laureate Daniel Kahneman noted: "We're blind to our blindness. We have very little idea of how little we know. We're not designed to know how little we know." And the problem starts very early in life: Even infants show an unconscious preference for more attractive people, fixating their eyes longer on people who are deemed more beautiful by other adults, and trusting those people more.[16]

So, while we should care about our unconscious or implicit biases, there is little scientific evidence in support of the idea that making people aware of their biases will eliminate problematic behaviors against the object of such biases, or reduce bias in general. In fact, a recent meta-analysis of 426 independent scientific studies with over 72,000 participants showed that unconscious bias interventions produce relatively small changes in implicit attitudes, and that such changes rarely translate into changes in explicit beliefs or actual behaviors.[17] As the authors concluded: "Together, these findings suggest that implicit bias is malleable, but that changing implicit bias does not necessarily lead to changes in explicit bias or behavior." When it comes to prejudiced and stereotypical biases, we must remember that they are mostly explicit rather than implicit, and conscious rather than unconscious. Most people are not just aware of their prejudiced biases, they are also proud of them: This is how they reap the main benefit from such biases, which is to feel better about themselves (by belittling other people). It is also questionable whether depriving people from that benefit will make them less angry, let alone more rational.

Importantly, it is not easy to consciously control unconscious thoughts, which is why the process often backfires.[18] Imagine we are training an interviewer, let's call him Donald, to overcome his unconscious biases against a certain group of people, such as women. Donald may undergo a great deal of training to identify his unconscious biases and finally accept the fact that he is a misogynist. But even if he had the best intention to keep such toxic attitudes in check when he is interviewing job candidates, that is a nearly impossible task: It would require him to ignore the gender of the person he is facing. In fact, the louder his inner voice tells him that he "should not pay attention to the candidate's gender," the more he will actually focus on that, at the expense of everything else. Although AI often gets a bad rap, it is far more likely—than human intelligence or intuition—to debias the assessment of humans. AI has two big advantages over human beings. First, unlike humans, AI can learn to ignore certain things, such as gender (which, in effect, means *unlearning certain categories*). Second, unlike humans, AI doesn't care about maintaining a positive self-view (and failing to maintain one will not make it depressed, since it has no self-esteem to protect). Indeed, even if AI continues to develop and upgrade itself, it can never be biased in a human way. For example, AI does not have a fragile self-esteem that it needs to inflate by bringing other people— or perhaps algorithms—down in order to feel validated. A neurotic or insecure AI may be a good idea for a *Black Mirror* episode, but a very bad technological solution.

Last, but not least, it is generally easier to identify our own rather than other people's biases, which includes stereotypes and prejudices. Indeed, you are more aware of your own prejudices over those of others, even when they seem more obvious than your own (an illusion that is itself a form of bias). That said, what matters most is not how *you* feel about your biases, but what *other* people think of them. You might be the least biased person in the world, but could still have a reputation for being biased, if your behaviors suggest that, or other people make a biased interpretation of how you behave. By the same token, you may have horrible internal biases, but behave in the least biased of ways vis-a-vis the subjects of such biases. Of course, sometimes there will be an alignment between your internal beliefs and external behaviors, which is something most people praise under the label of "authenticity," though being authentically racist or sexist is hardly a virtue. Remember what the key point here is: What matters most is what other people think of you. Whether or not you have a reputation for being biased is the critical issue at stake.

Respect, tolerance, and rational compassion

The big paradox underlying the D&I-authenticity connection is that if you must actually tell people that they are free to be themselves and behave authentically, they probably don't feel that it's actually safe to do so. In other words, in a truly inclusive culture where even outgroup individuals felt psychologically safe, it would be unnecessary for leaders or HR to nudge people to be themselves, let alone mandate how employees ought to behave, even if the mandate is assumed to represent a theoretical improvement over the status quo. In fact, what makes people feel more authentic at work, or at least have a sense of belonging with their employer, is to be given more autonomy and resources to do their job, which requires trust, support, and competent leadership, rather than telling people to bring their whole self to work.

Crucially, D&I interventions are more likely to improve behavior, not by making outgroup employees less interested in what others think of them, but by making ingroup employees more concerned about their own reputation. This would create some incentive for them to be more other-oriented, and more focused on displaying pro-social behaviors, particularly in practicing tolerance, kindness, and compassion. In other words, organizational cultures are more likely to improve not by forcing outgroup individuals to just be themselves, but by convincing ingroup individuals to stop being themselves. In turn, people who have historically been the target of prejudice and discrimination may start to experience more freedoms and fewer constraints on their behaviors—but tolerance must come first, and it must be real, in the sense of being a visible cultural tenet, rather than a formal imperative with little substance or safety behind it, or a moral aspiration nobody cares about.

Consider how this manifests with respect to gender. In many organizations, women are not just told to be authentic, be themselves, etc., but also encouraged to "lean in," show confidence, and be assertive, all of which is of course incompatible with the notion of being authentic. In contrast, men are not really told how to behave, which illustrates that they are given license to act however they want, including authentically. To make matters worse, when women try to conform to the behavioral guidelines imposed on them—apparently for their own benefit—they actually pay a price either for not being authentic, or because such behaviors are usually considered masculine and outside the traditional female stereotype.[19] So, while women are told how to behave, which involves a perverse combination of telling them to *be* and to *not* be themselves, men get away with murder, all courtesy of having no instructions, imperatives, or commands on improving their behaviors—they are fine as they are, while women need fixing. Unsurprisingly, toxic, antisocial, and dark side work behaviors are more often associated with male rather than female employees.[20]

Tolerance is largely about making compromises and sacrifices, as well as not being ourselves, particularly when we are tempted to disrespect or confront others, because the focus and goal of tolerance is to inhibit our own impulsive and authentic self-expression in order to make a valuable contribution to team harmony. Even in today's age of performance-obsessed organizations, it should be remembered that the definition of job performance anywhere and everywhere includes not just task performance (people accomplishing the various tasks that are formally outlined in their job description or yearly objectives), but also organizational citizenship (people behaving like responsible adults and making an effort to be kind and rewarding to deal with).[21] Fundamentally, organizational citizenship is about being a good employee and a good manager, taking care of not just your own, but other people's needs as well. It's about displaying prosocial rather than antisocial behaviors, and acting in the best interest of the organization or collective. Inevitably, this will mean making self-sacrifices, including censoring yourself, engaging in polite or civil interactions with others, and acting professionally (differently, for example, from how you would probably act when you are vacationing with your family, best friends, or partner/spouse, all of whom, incidentally, may appreciate the opportunity to hang out with your professional self after lengthy interactions with your uninhibited and personal self).

Cultures that foster a sense of civility, as well as a climate of tolerance, tend to condemn and sanction antisocial behaviors, regardless of whether these are authentic.[22] They will make an effort to police aggressions, reject any intolerance, and work hard to make outgroup employees feel included and limit the abuses of power by the ingroup. This is what Plato was alluding to when he pointed out that there can be no functioning society unless the rich and powerful are somewhat afraid of the poor. While even the more extreme instances of bad behavior—such as sexual harassment, bullying, intimidation, and corruption—may stem from their perpetrators' corrupt values, they will also be augmented by toxic cultures, which are unable or unwilling to sanction and suppress these bad behaviors.[23]

So, rather than allowing people to unleash their toxic behaviors, which are an expression of their authentic selves, they must instead act firmly and consistently to inhibit these acts, so that other people can feel safe and able to do their job. A certain degree of intolerance is needed to foster a climate of tolerance, since allowing anything will harness a culture of intolerance, where intolerant people can thrive. Conversely, where intolerance is condemned, outgroup individuals may feel safe to behave without any fear of repercussions, and without needing to be told that they can be themselves. After all, if somebody needs to tell you that you can be yourself, it is probably not evident that you can. Trust (not formal permission) and psychological safety (not en vogue management fads) are what unshackles underprivileged humans from the oppressive rules of the privileged elite.

It is also more feasible to focus less on what people believe deep down, or on who they *really* are (which would include their personal self and many other aspects of self-complexity not pertinent to the workplace), and more on what they actually do when they are at work. Instead of trying to police people's thoughts, change their beliefs, or expect the majority of humans to be naturally open to embracing those who have radically different backgrounds, interests, and values (which definitely won't happen if you persuade everybody to be true to their own values and expect others to adapt to them), a better way to improve D&I initiatives is to create a culture of respect, tolerance, and civility. In this culture, people will learn to go against their instincts and nature, and accept others in a way that comes across as authentic, but it will require a great deal of effort, practice, and method acting!

Amid much talk and praise for empathy—the old name for emotional intelligence—it should be noted that even empathy isn't sufficient to foster D&I, and that even kindness requires going beyond your authentic self. Paul Bloom, a best-selling psychologist and professor at Yale University, offers a nuanced critique of empathy, arguing that it can inadvertently harm diversity and foster division rather than unity. Note that empathy evolved as a primordial adaptation that rewards prioritizing genetic relatives and members of our inner tribe over strangers or diverse individuals. We are much more likely to experience empathy (feeling what others feel) for people who are like us, and therefore less likely to experience empathy for those who seem different (other races, genders, nationalities, etc.). In line, empathy is biased, leading us to favor individuals who are similar to us or whose sufferings are more vivid and immediate. This inclination can exacerbate divisions based on race, ethnicity, or nationality, as we're naturally drawn to empathize more with those who resemble us or our immediate social circle. By definition, if we have to feel empathy in order to be nice or act prosocially then the recipients of our niceness will disproportionately be people like us, which basically harms D&I. As such, empathy's discriminatory selectiveness undermines efforts to address systemic problems affecting diverse groups. Instead, Bloom advocates for "rational compassion" as a superior alternative to empathy. Rational compassion involves a more detached, principled approach to caring about others, one that relies on reason rather than emotion. This approach enables us to consider the needs of the many, rather than the few, and to make more equitable decisions about who to help and how. By adopting a stance of rational compassion, we're better equipped to address the root causes of inequality and suffering, and to make decisions that benefit a wider array of people without being swayed by emotional biases.

Bloom's critique is grounded in the idea that while empathy can motivate us to act, its narrow focus and inherent biases can lead to parochialism and a neglect of broader societal issues. Rational compassion, by contrast, encourages a more inclusive, equitable approach to alleviating suffering and promoting diversity. In other words, empathy can only get us so far: We feel empathy or intuitive feelings of compassion toward people who are naturally close to us—in genetic makeup, values, nationality, ethnicity, etc. So, even if you express empathy or let your empathy drive your prosocial behaviors, this will limit you to people who are like you. In that sense, empathy is a bit narcissistic because loving others who are like you is a subliminal and socially acceptable way to love yourself. Instead, rational compassion—which requires stepping outside your values, intuition, and authentic self—can help you be kind and nice to people who are different from you. A society where this happens at scale is much better than one in which only empathy rules (though that is still better than one with no empathy whatsoever).

Perhaps more worryingly, the same organizations that are vocally committed to D&I and authenticity also tend to embrace hiring for "culture fit," which, by definition, is incompatible with D&I strategies, not to mention authenticity. If culture is broadly defined as "how we do things around here" (i.e., the formal and informal rules of interaction that determine what's sanctioned and rewarded), then the people who "fit in" naturally are bound to be part of the ingroup, status quo, or ruling elite. Even worse, associations with culture fit will often be made on the basis of profile similarities, as in "X reminds me of Y, who is a salient reference for our culture." Therefore, X will fit right in. Historically, these were the kind of biases you could get away with while conducting a job interview with someone you would consider hiring, along the lines of "Oh, you also support Manchester United?" or "I see you went to Harvard, too?"

Nowadays, there is more precaution taken when designing hiring and selection processes so as to tame or extinguish biases, including during the job interview. However, "hiring for culture fit" still has a positive connotation, as in: "It's all about values and personal needs and drivers, so hiring on culture fit is a great way to cater to who you really are if you come here." Sounds nice, but it automatically excludes those who don't fit in. If you want a strong culture, you could end up with a cult, a homogeneous system in which people have such a strong sense of belonging that they are defined by their work persona, which, by definition, repels and rejects diversity as a value. The strongest cultures are not homogeneous cults, but diverse cultures where misfits are able to thrive, and when they do, they strengthen the culture by amplifying, enriching, and diversifying it. Diverse cultures evolve because they allow for a healthy tension between ingroup and outgroup values and behaviors, allowing for the best and most impactful ideas to win.

Furthermore, what if outgroup employees feel the need to *separate* their work and personal identities—hoping they can keep their unconventional or minority preferences, background, and values private—precisely because they are interested in fitting in, as opposed to standing out? Respecting people's need for privacy, as well as their desire to see work as what it is (namely work), would be a better D&I strategy than forcing them to share their intimate lives with others, particularly when they are not open-minded enough to understand or embrace individual differences, let alone group differences.

If managers, leaders, and bosses create a climate of psychological safety in their teams, then they won't need to tell people that they can bring their whole self or be authentic. In fact, doing so would be redundant or distasteful. Safety happens at the team and organizational level if people understand that there are limits to what they can say and do, while also knowing that it's worth taking the risk of speaking up when they must express themselves, particularly if there's a good reason for it—and that reason ought not to be selfish, but altruistic. If you create conditions for people to feel free to express themselves—which involves setting boundaries, safeguard, and rules, precisely so people can express themselves without repercussions—then you don't need to push people to be themselves or authentic.

Finally, despite good intentions, when organizations embrace authenticity as a key part of their D&I approach, they fail to address the fundamental reality that work does not automatically cater to all of our selves, that our identity is more than just our work or career persona, and that our whole self may not even be welcome at work. In fact, it is rare to have our whole selves welcome even at home. In my case, for instance, I experience a clear range of negative signals whenever I try to express specific aspects of my identity that are not welcome at home:

comfortable me, who refuses to unload the dishwasher, take out the rubbish, recycle, or only use his own toothbrush; *inflexible me,* who only picks his own choices on Netflix and Apple TV, forcing others to watch the same; or *irritable me,* who loses his sh-- as soon as someone touches his stuff, finishes the milk but doesn't replace it, or wakes him up when he's trying to sleep. If my whole self was welcome at home, all these habits, which are emblematic of my unedited and unfiltered identity and character, should not be censored or sanctioned. And, just as I need not find another home, relationship, or family who would put up with these obnoxious aspects of my personality, the notion that you need to look for a different job when you cannot bring your whole self to work is not just unrealistic, but ludicrous.

. . .

This chapter critically examines the intersection of D&I initiatives and the promotion of authenticity in the workplace. While organizations increasingly champion authenticity as a strategy to foster inclusion and psychological safety, the chapter highlights the inherent contradictions and challenges of this approach. Authenticity is disproportionately encouraged among outgroup individuals—those who deviate from dominant cultural norms—often without addressing the structural and psychological barriers they face. The call to "be yourself" can feel more like an imposition than a privilege, particularly for individuals whose authenticity risks professional repercussions. Furthermore, research shows that self-monitoring, impression management, and conformity often remain essential for career advancement, especially for outgroup members, thus rendering the promise of authenticity misleading or even harmful.

This chapter also underscored the flawed assumption that promoting authenticity automatically fosters inclusion. True inclusivity requires creating environments where people feel genuinely safe to express themselves—not through verbal mandates, but through actions that demonstrate tolerance, respect, and civility. The chapter critiques the "say-do gap" in D&I efforts, where organizations often emphasize inclusion rhetorically, without implementing meaningful cultural changes. Moreover, the paradox of authenticity lies in its tendency to exacerbate individualism, which can undermine the collective harmony that effective D&I strategies seek to achieve.

The pursuit of D&I in the workplace must move beyond superficial calls for authenticity, and instead focus on fostering environments of trust, respect, and psychological safety. Authenticity, when misapplied, can reinforce power imbalances, isolate outgroup individuals, and create unrealistic expectations for conformity under the guise of self-expression. Instead, organizations should prioritize actions that nurture inclusivity by addressing structural inequities, fostering cultural sensitivity, and promoting rational compassion. True inclusion requires more than the celebration of individuality; it demands the creation of spaces where individuals, regardless of their background, can thrive as part of a collective effort toward shared goals. By emphasizing civility and mutual respect over unfiltered self-expression, organizations can balance the need for individual authenticity with the greater good of diversity and inclusion.

Conclusion

It is inherent in humans to ask—and subsequently try to answer—the question of *how* we should best *be*, and how we can best display our character and our humanity, in a way that is most beneficial to our goals and objectives. This ranges from the short-term and trivial challenge of persuading our colleagues to help us with a work task, to the more consequential long-term quest for a positive image, reputation, and fulfilling career—job interviews, client presentations, salary negotiations, and any competition for meaningful and exciting opportunities to grow and succeed. Unlike those made by squirrels, mice, or fish, our choices are vast, even when we are unaware of their consequences, or seemingly constrained by external demands or internal barriers.

Although mainstream Western culture, and increasingly all modern cultures, have become obsessed with the notion that the best choice is one that ignores what others think, there *is* a better way to go about our work lives—and our personal lives as well. It starts by embracing a more other-oriented and empathetic approach to human interaction, one that questions the conventional (and self-centered) wisdom surrounding the alleged values and virtues of just being ourselves, and challenges us to think critically about the role of authenticity versus skilled and effective impression management in social and professional settings. Authenticity, while perhaps well-intended in theory, can at times limit our potential and hinder our ability to adapt to situations and relationships, especially when taken too literally or to the extreme.

By shifting our perspective, beyond the assumption that others value our unfiltered or genuine self *per se* (just like we would, for some reason, value other people's authentic self-expression *per se*), we can unlock more effective strategies for navigating the complexities and cultural nuances of work and life. This approach, while less self-serving, comforting, or self-obsessed, empowers us to be more intentional about how we present ourselves, communicate, and connect with others. It allows us to balance sincerity with adaptability, personal values with professional demands, and emotional truth with strategic thinking. In doing so, we can become more effective—better performers who rise to challenges with an awareness of our limitations, better leaders who inspire trust and collaboration, and better coworkers who contribute meaningfully to shared goals. Ultimately, this shift can open up more possibilities for growth, success, and fulfillment.

The great David Bowie—who, aside from his extraordinary musical and creative talent, was famous for repeatedly reinventing his artistic persona, in effect morphing into a different character with every new album—was once asked by a reported who he *really* was, in the sense of which of his artistic personas best represented his true or authentic persona, or was closest to his personal sense of identity. His response was as cool and ingenious as his artistic inventions: "I am only the person the greatest number of people think I am."

Bowie was no psychologist, but his answer is a beautiful reminder of a science-backed rule those who champion authenticity would benefit from learning: What you think of yourself is of minor practical importance compared to what others think of you. This includes how authentic you think you are, or how likeable, effective, creative, smart, or annoying you think you are. Just as Bowie had the humility of suspending judgment about his reputation (which depended, and still depends, on what *others* think of him), so should you, dear reader, remember that the impact you have on this world, and your ability to achieve anything important that you may wish for, is far more dependent on how you are viewed by others, than on how you view yourself.

While others are generally of the opinion that it's better to interact with the genuine rather than fake version of yourself, they would much prefer interacting with your kind, polite, socially skilled, and selfless self—regardless of how much effort it takes for you to display this—than an authentic self who is self-centered, focused on its own values, interests, and objectives, and eager to impose its own views, ideals, and ideas on others (particularly when this implies it is the center of the universe).

As this book has hopefully illustrated, the main tenets underpinning the popular or mainstream notion of authenticity lead to this toxic approach to social interactions. This includes refraining from any filters and communicating your unsolicited views to others; disregarding what others think of you; never entertaining the fact that your values may not be superior to others; assuming that your work colleagues are somehow interested in every personal aspect of your identity, thoughts, and beliefs; and believing that there are no restrictions or boundaries to bringing your "whole self" to work, as if there were no difference between work and a carefree vacation with your closest friends.

Conversely, when you start to live your life and approach your work as an opportunity to express the best version of you—and by understanding that social interactions require compromises, flexibility, and adapting your "self" to the relevant demands of each situation—you will probably start making an effort to edit, constrain, and filter the spontaneous, natural, and uncensored version of yourself that is most closely associated with authenticity. To be sure, psychological maturity and interpersonal effectiveness are largely achieved when one can make an accurate reading of a situation, so as to display only the relevant aspects of one's identity and express the character traits that are demanded in that moment. The spoiled child within us will persist in being heard and unleashed, but it's the responsible grownup others hope to interact with, especially in a work setting.

Contrary to popular belief, there is a better path to career success than the "just be yourself" rule, which includes *not* being yourself, in the sense of avoiding the natural temptation we all face, particularly as we make progress in our professional and personal lives: becoming an exaggerated version of ourselves, indulging in the privilege of disregarding others and demanding that *they* adjust to our way of being, and becoming more like ourselves as time goes by. In fact, the more we resist this temptation, which starts by making an effort to be rewarding to deal with, to make a favorable impression on others, and to conceal the least desirable ingredients of our personality in any consequential interaction with others, the more we will be appreciated by others, and the more we will advance our careers. Indeed, the hallmark of psychological maturity lies in understanding that personal growth is an ongoing process of adaptation, refinement, and self-regulation. Success—particularly in interpersonal settings, which are basically any consequential situation where we have the chance to increase our status, success, and happiness—always requires you to balance or dilute authenticity with adaptability. This doesn't mean fully abandoning your core values or integrity, but rather learning to present those values in ways that resonate with and accommodate others (who ought not to be seen as your audience, but rather as an integral part of your behavioral script). In other words, to behave appropriately is to act as the situation demands, and the situation is, in essence, other people.

David Bowie's brilliance wasn't just in his artistic reinvention, but also in his ability to recognize that identity, like art, is interpretive.

Just as audiences saw facets of themselves in Bowie's personas, the people you interact with daily will interpret your character through their own filters, experiences, and expectations. Thus, the version of yourself you choose to show—how you communicate, collaborate, and compromise—becomes the bridge between your personal identity and others' perception of you. Furthermore, it is mostly others, not you, who assign meaning to your actions and personality, and this presents a wonderful opportunity to sculpt and shape your reputation in ways that go beyond your past behaviors, default dispositions, and tendencies, so as to become a more expanded, complex, and diverse version of yourself. Indeed, why limit yourself to who you are if you can also become who you haven't been yet? And why act according to your natural inclinations and habits if you can go beyond your comfort zone and expand the behavioral repertoire that constrains and limits your ordinary self? Seen in this way, authenticity becomes an attribution made by others—and not to when you are just being yourself, but to when you have learned to act in novel ways that are still genuine and believable to others (like the versatile method actor who isn't limited to playing the same kind of role over and over again).

Authenticity should not be about unrestrained self-expression or insisting on being fully understood on your own terms. Instead, it's about achieving harmony between self-expression and social connection. This means prioritizing the collective good over your self-indulgence, and recognizing that relationships—personal and professional—thrive on reciprocity, sacrifices, and shared purpose. To illustrate, think about the leaders, colleagues, or friends who have left a lasting and positive impression on you. They likely weren't the loudest or most uninhibited individuals, but rather those who made you feel valued, heard, and understood. They didn't dominate conversations with their opinions, but instead demonstrated an ability to listen, adapt, and engage thoughtfully. Their authenticity wasn't about oversharing their entire identity. It was about seeming sufficiently genuine in their intent and considerate in their actions, and worrying more about how you feel than unleashing their unfiltered self.

The ability to regulate and tailor your behavior to different contexts is not a betrayal of your true self, but rather a mark of emotional intelligence and interpersonal skill. It's not about faking who you are, but instead about showcasing the facets of yourself that best serve the situation and the people around you. Much like Bowie's ability to reinvent his artistic personas to suit the themes and times, you can reinvent aspects of yourself to align with the evolving demands of your career and relationships.

In sum, the key to advancing your career, unlocking your potential, and becoming your best self lies not in rigidly adhering to the idea of being your authentic self at all costs, but in embracing the fluidity of identity and making a concerted effort to curate and maintain a positive reputation. Strive to be the version of yourself that contributes meaningfully to the world around you—the version that listens, learns, adapts, and inspires, even if it means putting your whole self backstage. After all, the measure of a successful life isn't how steadfastly you remain unchanged, but how gracefully you evolve to meet the needs of the moment while managing to grow and develop for the long-term future.

In short, why be yourself when you can be someone better? Why be limited to your past and present self if you can also broaden your character, identity, and reputation by embracing your possible future selves, which requires you to act "out of character" and go against your nature? Why age like most people, who become a more exaggerated and rigid version of their earlier selves? Why remain true to your personal values and core beliefs, when you can question these values and beliefs with self-critical humility, and thus mature ethically and morally, enabling your values and beliefs to evolve and mature? Why think that, by remaining firm on your thoughts, beliefs, and feelings, you are somehow superior or admirable, when you could be open to other people's values, understand how they think and why they feel what they feel, and avoid the prevalent tribalization and polarization that affects most people, including those who regard themselves as open-minded (while curiously only hanging out with like-minded people)? And why unleash your uncensored and uninhibited self on others, instead of showing a modicum of consideration and kindness to others?

There is no prize for becoming who you already are, but there is a remarkable payoff for becoming a better version of yourself, including the admiration and respect of others. However, this requires some effort, focus, and dedication. Above all, it requires the motivation to seriously want to evolve, which is the exact opposite of just being yourself.

We are all unique, just like everybody else. And, just like everybody else, too, we would love to live in a world in which we are the center of the universe. However, that is unlikely to happen, even for Elon Musk, though he may get closer than anyone else to turning this delusion into a reality, even if it requires moving to a different planet (and Mars does not occupy a more central position in the universe than planet Earth). Consequently, understanding that we are part of a collective system, and that most enjoyable and productive things in life—including our major accomplishments and progress, not to mention our long-term wellness and happiness—are the result of our ability to dilute rather than inflate our egos in order to become part of something greater than ourselves, is perhaps the strongest argument for resisting the allure of the authenticity cult.

In the end, maybe the best life advice isn't "just be yourself," but rather "just be someone everyone else genuinely enjoys being around." Because, truthfully, if being authentically you means spontaneously sharing your political rants at company meetings, showcasing your interpretive dance skills during quarterly reviews, or proudly refusing deodorant because it "masks your true essence," you might quickly find yourself authentically unemployed and genuinely friendless. So yes, by all means, keep it real—just don't make everyone else suffer for it. Embrace your inner Bowie: Swap personas, expand your identity, and charm the crowd while you're at it. After all, life isn't about proving how authentically insufferable you can be, but about gracefully becoming someone whose absence is sincerely felt and whose presence genuinely celebrated—someone who understands that authenticity at its best isn't loudly insisting "this is who I am," but quietly inspiring others to say, "we're glad you're here."

Notes

Introduction

1. L. J. Goren, "Authenticity and Emotion: Hillary Rodham Clinton's Dual Constraints," *Politics and Gender* 14, Special Issue 1: Gender and Conservatism (March 2018): 111–115.

2. M. L. Osorio, E. Centeno, and J. Cambra-Fierro, "An Empirical Examination of Human Brand Authenticity as a Driver of Brand Love," *Journal of Business Research* 165, no. 1 (2023), https://doi.org/10.1016/j.jbusres.2023.114059.

3. L. Bunce and P. L. Harris, "Is It Real? The Development of Judgments About Authenticity and Ontological Status," *Cognitive Development* 32 (2014): 110–119.

4. A. Serenko, "The Human Capital Management Perspective on Quiet Quitting: Recommendations for Employees, Managers, and National Policymakers," *Journal of Knowledge Management* 28, no. 1 (2024): 27–43.

5. Brené Brown, *The Gifts of Imperfection: Let Go of Who You Think You're Supposed to Be and Embrace Who You Are* (Center City, MN: Hazelden, 2010).

6. Gabrielle Bernstein, *Judgment Detox: Release the Beliefs That Hold You Back from Living a Better Life* (New York: Simon & Schuster, 2018).

7. Robin S. Sharma, *The Monk Who Sold His Ferrari* (San Francisco: HarperSanFrancisco, 1999).

8. "Authentic: Merriam-Webster's Word of the Year," *BBC News*, November 27, 2023, https://www.bbc.com/news/world-us-canada-67543895.

9. "Review of The Complete Works of Oscar Wilde," *Choice Reviews Online*, 39, no. 11 (2001): 39-6311.

10. Fred R. Shapiro, ed., *The New Yale Book of Quotations* (New Haven, CT: Yale University Press, 2021).

11. Tomas Chamorro-Premuzic, *Confidence: Overcoming Low Self-Esteem, Insecurity, and Self-Doubt* (New York: Hudson Street Press, 2013); Tomas Chamorro-Premuzic, "Why Do So Many Incompetent Men Become Leaders?," *Harvard Business Review*, August 22, 2013, https://hbr.org/2013/08/why-do-so -many-incompetent-men; Tomas Chamorro-Premuzic, *I, Human: AI, Automation, and the Quest to Reclaim What Makes Us Unique* (Boston: Harvard Business Review Press, 2023).

12. Daniel J. Boorstin, *Life Quotes Notebook, Motivational Notebook, Journal, Diary* (self-pub., 2020).

13. G. Medlock, "The Evolving Ethic of Authenticity: From Humanistic to Positive Psychology," *Humanistic Psychologist* 40, no. 1 (2012): 38–57.

14. U. B. Metin, T. W. Taris, M. C. W. Peeters, I. van Beek, and R. van den Bosch, "Authenticity at Work—A Job-Demands Resources Perspective," *Journal of Managerial Psychology* 31, no. 2 (2016): 483–499.

15. B. Kuyumcu and A. Kabasakaloglu, "The Predictive Power of Authenticity on Emotional Well-Being (Positive-Negative Affect): Authenticity and Positive-Negative Affect Among Turkish and English University Students," *Journal of Higher Education and Science* 8, no. 1 (2018): 184–193; J. (Y.) Ma, A. R. Sachdev, and X. Gu, "Being Oneself and Doing Great: The Effect of Authenticity on Job Performance and the Role of Supportive Leadership," *Journal of Personnel Psychology* 19, no. 2 (2020): 75–85.

16. X. Chen, "Happiness and Authenticity: Confucianism and Heidegger," *Journal of Philosophical Research* 38, no. 2 (2013): 261–274; Z. G. Baker, R. Y. W. Tou, J. L. Bryan, and C. R. Knee, "Authenticity and Well-Being: Exploring Positivity and Negativity in Interactions as a Mediator," *Personality and Individual Differences* 113, no. 2 (2017): 235–239.

17. R. E. Wickham, "Perceived Authenticity in Romantic Partners," *Journal of Experimental Social Psychology* 49, no. 5 (2013): 878–887.

18. D. G. Pinto, J. Maltby, A. M. Wood, and L. Day, "A Behavioral Test of Horney's Linkage Between Authenticity and Aggression: People Living Authentically Are Less-Likely to Respond Aggressively in Unfair Situations," *Personality and Individual Differences* 52, no. 1 (2012): 41–44.

19. B. Kovács, "Authenticity Is in the Eye of the Beholder: The Exploration of Audiences' Lay Associations to Authenticity Across Five Domains," *Review of General Psychology* 23, no. 1 (2019): 32–59.

20. G. E. Newman and R. K. Smith, "Kinds of Authenticity," *Philosophy Compass* 11, no. 10 (2016): 609–618.

21. J. M. Twenge and J. D. Foster, "Birth Cohort Increases in Narcissistic Personality Traits Among American College Students, 1982–2009," *Social Psychological and Personality Science* 1, no. 1 (2010): 99–106.

22. J. M. Twenge, "Status and Gender: The Paradox of Progress in an Age of Narcissism," *Sex Roles* 61, no. 5 (2009): 338–340; J. M. Twenge, "A Review of the Empirical Evidence on Generational Differences in Work Attitudes," *Journal of Business and Psychology* 25, no. 2 (2010): 201–210.

23. O. P. John and R. W. Robins, "Accuracy and Bias in Self-Perception: Individual Differences in Self-Enhancement and the Role of Narcissism," *Journal of Personality and Social Psychology* 66, no. 1 (1994): 206–219.

Chapter 1

1. P. C. Regan, M. Snyder, and S. M. Kassin, "Unrealistic Optimism: Self-Enhancement or Person Positivity?" *Personality and Social Psychology Bulletin* 21, no. 10 (1995): 1073–1082.

2. R. W. Trollinger and J. R. Thelin, "The Greater Good," *Philanthropy & Education* 7, no. 1 (Fall 2023): 25–33.

3. A. Padilla, R. Hogan, and R. B. Kaiser, "The Toxic Triangle: Destructive Leaders, Susceptible Followers, and Conducive Environments," *Leadership Quarterly* 18, no. 3 (2007): 176–194.

4. R. Barkan, S. Ayal, and D. Ariely, "Ethical Dissonance, Justifications, and Moral Behavior," *Current Opinion in Psychology* 6 (2015): 157–161.

5. S. Ayal and F. Gino, "Honest Rationales for Dishonest Behavior," in *The Social Psychology of Morality: Exploring the Causes of Good and Evil*, eds. Mario Mikulincer and Phillip R. Shaver (Washington, DC: American Psychological Association, 2011), 149–166.

6. A. C. Homan, C. Buengeler, R. A. Eckhoff, W. P. van Ginkel, and S. C. Voelpel, "The Interplay of Diversity Training and Diversity Beliefs on Team Creativity in Nationality Diverse Teams," *Journal of Applied Psychology* 100, no. 5 (2015): 1456–1467.

7. W. Krämer, "Kahneman, D. (2011): Thinking, Fast and Slow," *Statistical Papers* 55 (2014): 915.

8. J. Polivy and C. P. Herman, "The False-Hope Syndrome: Unfulfilled Expectations of Self-Change," *Current Directions in Psychological Science* 9, no. 4 (2000): 128–131.

9. D. L. Ryan, "Paul Bloom: Against Empathy: The Case for Rational Compassion," *Society* 55, no. 2 (2018): 216–217.

10. C. H. Cooley, *Human Nature and the Social Order* (New York: Routledge, 2017).

11. Anthony Wilden, "Death and Narcissism: The Solipsist and the Salauds," in *System and Structure: Essays in Communication and Exchange*, 2nd ed. (New York: Tavistock, 1980), 468–471.

12. C. L. Exley and J. B. Kessler, "Psychological Conditions of Personal Engagement and Disengagement at Work" (working paper 26345, National Bureau of Economic Research, 2019), http://www.nber.org/papers/w26345.

13. A. R. McConnell, L. M. Strain, C. M. Brown, and R. J. Rydell, "The Simple Life: On the Benefits of Low Self-Complexity," *Personality and Social Psychology Bulletin* 35, no. 7 (2009): 823–835.

14. L. Garrad and T. Chamorro-Premuzic, "The Dark Side of High Employee Engagement," *Harvard Business Review*, August 16, 2016, https://hbr.org/2016/08/the-dark-side-of-high-employee-engagement.

15. M. Hennigan and L. Evans, "Does Hiring for 'Culture Fit' Perpetuate Bias?" Society for Human Resource Management, October 31, 2018, https://www.shrm.org/mena/topics-tools/news/hr-magazine/hiring-culture-fit-perpetuate-bias.

16. T. Chamorro-Premuzic, "Seven Rules for Managing Creative-but-Difficult People," *Harvard Business Review*, April 2, 2013, https://hbr.org/2013/04/seven-rules-for-managing-creat.

17. R. Hogan, G. J. Curphy, and J. Hogan, "What We Know About Leadership: Effectiveness and Personality," *American Psychologist* 49, no. 6 (1994): 493–504.

Chapter 2

1. H.G. Moeller and P. J. D'Ambrosio, "Sincerity, Authenticity and Profilicity: Notes on the Problem, a Vocabulary and a History of Identity," *Philosophy and Social Criticism* 45, no. 5 (2019): 575–596.

2. J. Butterworth, R. Trivers, and W. von Hippel, "The Better to Fool You With: Deception and Self-Deception," *Current Opinion in Psychology* 47 (2022), https://doi.org/10.1016/j.copsyc.2022.101385.

3. R. Trivers, "The Elements of a Scientific Theory of Self-Deception," *Annals of the New York Academy of Sciences* 907, no. 1 (2000): 114–131.

4. C. Kennedy-Pipe and R. Vickers, "'Blowback' for Britain?: Blair, Bush, and the War in Iraq," *Review of International Studies* 33, no. 2 (2007): 205–221.

5. A. A. Boni and S. M. Sammut, "'The Good, the Bad, the Ugly': Leadership Lessons from Two Companies—Amgen and Theranos," *Journal of Commercial Biotechnology* 24, no. 4 (2019), https://doi.org/10.5912/JCB918.

6. B. Leavy, "Startups—Tom Eisenmann Analyzes the Most Prevalent Failure Patterns and How to Avoid Them," *Strategy and Leadership* 49, no. 5 (2021): 31–37.

7. N. Mazar, O. Amir, and D. Ariely, "The Dishonesty of Honest People: A Theory of Self-Concept Maintenance," *Journal of Marketing Research* 45, no. 6 (2008): 633–644.

8. M. P. Wilmot, D. S. Ones, and J. E. Barbuto, "A Meta-Analytic Structural Model of Self-Monitoring, Interpersonal Effectiveness, and Status at Work" (paper presented at the 79th Annual Meeting of the Academy of Management, August 2019), https://doi:10.5465/AMBPP.2019.74.

9. L. Friedman, "Optimal Bluffing Strategies in Poker," *Management Science* 17, no. 12 (1971): 764–771.

10. K. Lee, "Little Liars: Development of Verbal Deception in Children," *Child Development Perspectives* 7, no. 2 (2013): 91–96.

11. T. Chamorro-Premuzic, "Thriving in the Age of Hybrid Work," *Harvard Business Review*, January 13, 2021, https://hbr.org/2021/01/thriving-in-the-age-of-hybrid-work.

12. T. Chamorro-Premuzic and K. Berg, "Fostering a Culture of Belonging in the Hybrid Workplace," *Harvard Business Review*, August 3, 2021, https://hbr.org/2021/08/fostering-a-culture-of-belonging-in-the-hybrid-workplace.

13. A. Nehamas, "Nietzsche on Truth and the Value of Falsehood," *Journal of Nietzsche Studies* 48, no. 3 (2017): 319–346.

14. F. Anderson, L. Salamo, and B. L. Stein, *Mark Twain's Notebooks and Journals, Volume II: 1877–1883* (Oakland: University of California Press, 2023).

15. L. Uziel, "Rethinking Social Desirability Scales: From Impression Management to Interpersonally Oriented Self-Control," *Perspectives on Psychological Science* 5, no. 3 (2010): 243–262.

16. A. A. Grandey, G. M. Fisk, A. S. Mattila, K. J. Jansen, and L. A. Sideman, "Is 'Service with a Smile' Enough? Authenticity of Positive Displays During Service Encounters," *Organizational Behavior and Human Decision Processes* 96, no. 1 (2005): 38–55.

17. D. Delpechitre and L. Beeler, "Faking It: Salesperson Emotional Intelligence's Influence on Emotional Labor Strategies and Customer Outcomes," *Journal of Business and Industrial Marketing* 33, no. 1 (2018): 53–71.

18. T. Chamorro-Premuzic and M. Sanger, "How to Boost Your (and Others') Emotional Intelligence," *Harvard Business Review*, January 19, 2017, https://hbr.org/2017/01/how-to-boost-your-and-others-emotional -intelligence.

19. N. Brody, "What Cognitive Intelligence Is and What Emotional Intelligence Is Not," *Psychological Inquiry* 15, no. 3 (2004): 234–238.

20. D. van der Linden, K. A. Pekaar, A. B. Bakker, J. A. Schermer, P. A. Vernon, C. S. Dunkel, and K. V. Petrides, "Overlap Between the General Factor of Personality and Emotional Intelligence: A Meta-Analysis," *Psychological Bulletin* 143, no. 1 (2016): 36–52.

21. R. Hogan, T. Chamorro-Premuzic, and R. B. Kaiser, "Employability and Career Success: Bridging the Gap Between Theory and Reality," *Industrial and Organizational Psychology* 6 (2013): 3–16.

22. M. Bolino, D. Long, and W. Turnley, "Impression Management in Organizations: Critical Questions, Answers, and Areas for Future Research," *Annual Review of Organizational Psychology and Organizational Behavior* 3, no. 1 (2016): 377–406.

23. R. A. Griggs, "Coverage of the Phineas Gage Story in Introductory Psychology Textbooks: Was Gage No Longer Gage?" *Teaching of Psychology* 42, no. 3 (2015): 195–202.

24. P. Ratiu, I. F. Talos, S. Haker, D. Lieberman, and P. Everett, "The Tale of Phineas Gage, Digitally Remastered," *Journal of Neurotrauma* 21, no. 5 (2004): 637–643.

25. J. Posner, "Erving Goffman: His Presentation of Self," *Philosophy of the Social Sciences* 8, no. 1 (1978): 67–78.

26. D. Gross, "Bridgewater May Be the Hottest Hedge Fund for Harvard Grads," *Daily Beast*, March 7, 2013, https://www.thedailybeast.com /bridgewater-may-be-the-hottest-hedge-fund-for-harvard-grads-but-its -also-the-weirdest.

27. M. Gimein, "Ever Had a Horrible Boss? 'The Fund' Is the Perfect Rage-Read," review of *The Fund*, by Rob Copeland, *New York Times*, November 6, 2013, https://www.nytimes.com/2023/11/06/books/review/the -fund-rob-copeland.html.

28. Rob Copeland, *The Fund: Ray Dalio, Bridgewater Associates, and the Unraveling of a Wall Street Legend* (New York: St. Martin's Press, 2023).

29. J. Friedrichs, "Useful Lies: The Twisted Rationality of Denial," *Philosophical Psychology* 27, no. 2 (2014): 212–234.

30. S. A. Andrzejewski and E. C. Mooney, "Service with a Smile: Does the Type of Smile Matter?" *Journal of Retailing and Consumer Services* 29, no. 1 (2016): 135–141.

31. R. H. Humphrey, B. E. Ashforth, and J. M. Diefendorff, "The Bright Side of Emotional Labor," *Journal of Organizational Behavior* 36, no. 6 (2015): 749–769.

32. "Should You Be Nice at Work," *Economist*, September 19, 2024, https://www.economist.com/business/2024/09/19/should-you-be-nice-at-work.

33. A. B. Blake, V. H. Luu, O. V. Petrenko, W. L. Gardner, K. J. N. Moergen, and M. E. Ezerins, "Let's Agree About Nice Leaders: A Literature Review and Meta-Analysis of Agreeableness and Its Relationship with Leadership Outcomes," *Leadership Quarterly* 33, no. 1 (2022): 1–23.

34. A. Kim, "Follow the Leader: How a CEO's Personality Is Reflected in Their Company's Culture," Graduate School of Stanford Business, August 1, 2023, https://www.gsb.stanford.edu/insights/follow-leader-how-ceos-personality-reflected-their-companys-culture.

35. M. Bolino, D. Long, and W. Turnley, "Impression Management in Organizations: Critical Questions, Answers, and Areas for Future Research," *Annual Review of Organizational Psychology and Organizational Behavior* 3, no. 1 (2016): 377–406.

36. P. W. L. Vlaar, F. A. J. van den Bosch, and H. W. Volberda, "On the Evolution of Trust, Distrust, and Formal Coordination and Control in Interorganizational Relationships: Toward an Integrative Framework," *Group & Organization Management* 32, no. 4 (2007): 407–428.

37. A. Guttman, "These 3 Things Predict Success in Fund-Raising Pitches, Says Harvard Psychologist," *Forbes*, March 31, 2016, https://www.forbes.com/sites/amyguttman/2016/03/31/harvard-psychologist-finds-3-things-predict-success-in-fund-raising-pitches.

Chapter 3

1. V. Messing and B. Ságvári, "Are Anti-Immigrant Attitudes the Holy Grail of Populists? A Comparative Analysis of Attitudes Towards Immigrants, Values, and Political Populism in Europe," *Intersections. East European Journal of Society and Politics* 7, no. 2 (2021): 100–127.

2. S. L. Gillan, A. Koch, and L. T. Starks, "Firms and Social Responsibility: A Review of ESG and CSR Research in Corporate Finance," *Journal of Corporate Finance* 66, no. 3 (2021), https://doi.org/10.1016/j.jcorpfin.2021.101889.

3. S. D. Schaefer, R. Terlutter, and S. Diehl, "Is My Company Really Doing Good? Factors Influencing Employees' Evaluation of the Authenticity of Their Company's Corporate Social Responsibility Engagement," *Journal of Business Research* 101 (2019): 128–143.

4. A. Mirzaei, D. C. Wilkie, and H. Siuki, "Woke Brand Activism Authenticity or the Lack of It," *Journal of Business Research* 139, no. 3 (2022): 1–12.

5. S. Alhouti, C. M. Johnson, and B. B. Holloway, "Corporate Social Responsibility Authenticity: Investigating Its Antecedents and Outcomes," *Journal of Business Research* 69, no. 3 (2016): 1242–1249.

6. G. J. Hitsch, A. Hortaçsu, and D. Ariely, "What Makes You Click? Mate Preferences in Online Dating," *Quantitative Marketing and Economics* 8 no. 4 (2010): 1–35.

7. A. J. Villado and W. Arthur, Jr., "The Comparative Effect of Subjective and Objective After-Action Reviews on Team Performance on a Complex Task," *Journal of Applied Psychology* 98, no. 3 (2013): 514–528.

8. A. J. Bingham, W. Durant, and A. Durant, "Review of *The Age of Voltaire*," *Modern Language Journal* 50, no. 7 (1966): 498–500.

9. Karl Popper and Vaclav Havel, *The Open Society and Its Enemies* (London: Routledge, 2012).

10. Jonathan Haidt, *The Righteous Mind: Why Good People Are Divided by Politics and Religion* (New York: Pantheon, 2012).

11. J. Haidt, "Moral Psychology for the Twenty-First Century," *Journal of Moral Education* 42, no. 3 (2013): 281–297.

Chapter 4

1. I.-S. Oh, R. P. Guay, K. Kim, C. M. Harold, J.-H. Lee, C.-G. Heo, and K.-H. Shin, "Fit Happens Globally: A Meta-Analytic Comparison of the Relationships of Person-Environment Fit Dimensions with Work Attitudes and Performance Across East Asia, Europe, and North America," *Personnel Psychology* 67, no. 1 (2014): 99–152.

2. O. George, O. Owoyemi, and U. Onakala, "Hofstede's 'Software of the Mind' Revisited and Tested: The Case of Cadbury Worldwide and Cadbury (Nigeria) Plc - A Qualitative Study," *International Business Research* 5, no. 9 (2012): 148–157.

3. G. Ahmetoglu, X. Harding, R. Akhtar, and T. Chamorro-Premuzic, "Predictors of Creative Achievement: Assessing the Impact of Entrepreneurial Potential, Perfectionism, and Employee Engagement," *Creative Research Journal* 27, no. 2 (2015), 198–205.

4. J. C. Kaufman, "Individual Differences in Creativity," in *The Wiley-Blackwell Handbook of Individual Differences*, eds. Tomas Chamorro-Premuzic, Sophie von Stumm, and Adrian Furnham (Hoboken, NJ: Wiley-Blackwell, 2013), 679–697.

5. R. van Wijk, J. Jansen, and M. Lyles, "Social Capital, Knowledge Transfer and Performance: Meta-Analytic Evidence," *Academy of Management Proceedings* 2008, no. 1 (2008): 1–6.

6. T. R. Cohen, A. T. Panter, N. Turan, L. Morse, and Y. Kim, "Moral Character in the Workplace," *Journal of Personality and Social Psychology* 107, no. 5 (2014): 943–963.

7. J. Piaget, "Part I: Cognitive Development in Children—Piaget Development and Learning," *Journal of Research in Science Teaching* 2 (1964): 176–186.

8. H. Borke, "Piaget's Mountains Revisited: Changes in the Egocentric Landscape," *Developmental Psychology* 11, no. 2 (1975): 240–243.

9. I. Morris, "Turchin, Peter. Ultrasociety: How 10,000 Years of War Made Humans the Greatest Cooperators on Earth," *Evolutionary Studies in Imaginative Culture* 1, no. 2 (2017): 1–14.

10. Karen Dillon, *HBR Guide to Office Politics* (Brighton, MA: Harvard Business Review Press, 2014).

11. J. McCrone, "Feral Children," *Lancet Neurology* 2, no. 2 (2003): 132.

12. Jane Yolen, *Children of the Wolf* (New York: Viking Press, 1984).

13. A. L. Glowinski and T. E. Spiegel, "Cinephilic Survival and Transcendence," *PsycCRITIQUES* 61, no. 4 (2016), http://dx.doi.org/10.1037/a0040081.

14. S. K. Jacobson and M. D. Mcduff, "Training Idiot Savants: The Lack of Human Dimensions in Conservation Biology," *Conservation Biology* 12, no. 2 (1998): 263–267.

15. D. A. Treffert, "The Savant Syndrome: An Extraordinary Condition. A Synopsis: Past, Present, Future," *Philosophical Transactions of the Royal Society B: Biological Sciences* 364, no. 1522 (2009): 1351–1357.

16. J. B. Hittner and R. Swickert, "Sensation Seeking and Alcohol Use: A Meta-Analytic Review," *Addictive Behaviors* 31, no. 8 (2006): 1383–1401.

17. R. B. Kaiser, J. M. Lebreton, and J. Hogan, "The Dark Side of Personality and Extreme Leader Behavior," *Applied Psychology* 64, no. 1 (2013): 55–92.

18. Kate Fox, *Watching the English: The Hidden Rules of English Behaviour* (London: Hodder, 2004).

19. M. D. Barnett and K. J. Sharp, "Narcissism, Gender, and Evolutionary Theory: The Role of Private and Public Self-Absorption," *Personality and Individual Differences* 104 (2017): 326–332.

20. Simon Baron-Cohen, *The Science of Evil: On Empathy and the Origins of Cruelty* (New York: Basic Books, 2011).

21. D. L. Paulhus and K. M. Williams, "The Dark Triad of Personality: Narcissism, Machiavellianism, and Psychopathy," *Journal of Research in Personality* 36, no. 6 (2002): 556–563.

22. S. Baron-Cohen and S. Wheelwright, "The Empathy Quotient: An Investigation of Adults with Asperger Syndrome or High Functioning Autism, and Normal Sex Differences," *Journal of Autism and Developmental Disorders* 34, no. 2 (2004): 163–175.

23. A. N. Kluger and G. Itzchakov, "The Power of Listening at Work," *Annual Review of Organizational Psychology and Organizational Behavior* 9, no. 1 (2002): 121–146.

24. C. K. W. de Dreu, "Cooperative Outcome Interdependence, Task Reflexivity, and Team Effectiveness: A Motivated Information Processing Perspective," *Journal of Applied Psychology* 92, no. 3 (2007): 628–638.

25. J. B. Grubbs, J. J. Exline, J. B. Grubbs, and J. J. Exline, "Trait Entitlement: A Cognitive-Personality Source of Vulnerability to Psychological Distress," *Psychological Bulletin* 142, no. 11 (2016): 1204–1226.

26. F.-M. Hartung and B. Renner, "Social Curiosity and Interpersonal Perception: A Judge x Trait Interaction," *Personality and Social Psychology Bulletin* 37, no. 6 (2011): 796–814.

27. L. E. Atwater and F. J. Yammarino, "Does Self-Other Agreement on Leadership Perceptions Moderate the Validity of Leadership and Performance Predictions?" *Personnel Psychology* 45, no. 1 (1992): 141–164.

28. G. Millar, "Employee Engagement—A New Paradigm," *Human Resource Management International Digest* 20, no. 2 (2012): 3–5.

29. Henry David Thoreau, *Walden* (Las Vegas: Empire Books, 2012).

30. Allan H. Church, David W. Bracken, John W. Fleenor, and Dale S. Rose, *Handbook of Strategic 360 Feedback* (New York: Oxford University Press, 2019).

31. Gordon W. Allport, *The Nature of Prejudice* (Reading, MA: Addison-Wesley, 1954).

32. K. A. Ericsson, "Deliberate Practice and Acquisition of Expert Performance: A General Overview," *Academic Emergency Medicine* 15, no. 11 (2008): 988–994.

33. J. A. Brooks, R. M. Stolier, and J. B. Freeman, "Computational Approaches to the Neuroscience of Social Perception," *Social Cognitive and Affective Neuroscience* 16, no. 8 (2021): 827–837.

34. N. O. Rule and N. Ambady, "Face and Fortune: Inferences of Personality from Managing Partners' Faces Predict Their Law Firms' Financial Success," *Leadership Quarterly* 22, no. 4 (2011): 690–696.

35. J. Pillemer, E. R. Graham, and D. M. Burke, "The Face Says It All: CEOs, Gender, and Predicting Corporate Performance," *Leadership Quarterly* 25, no. 5 (2014): 855–864.

36. J. L. Tackett, K. Herzhoff, S. C. Kushner, and N. Rule, "Thin Slices of Child Personality: Perceptual, Situational, and Behavioral Contributions," *Journal of Personality and Social Psychology* 110, no. 1 (2016): 150–166.

37. S. Davidai and T. Gilovich, "The Headwinds/Tailwinds Asymmetry: An Availability Bias in Assessments of Barriers and Blessings," *Journal of Personality and Social Psychology* 111, no. 6 (2016): 835–851.

38. J. H. Langlois, L. Kalakanis, A. J. Rubenstein, A. Larson, M. Hallam, and M. Smoot, "Maxims or Myths of Beauty? A Meta-Analytic and Theoretical Review," *Psychological Bulletin* 126, no. 3 (2000): 390–423.

39. C. Nater and E. Zell, "Accuracy of Social Perception: An Integration and Review of Meta-Analyses," *Social and Personality Psychology Compass* 9, no. 9 (2015): 481–494.

40. P. Borkenau, N. Mauer, R. Riemann, F. M. Spinath, and A. Angleitner, "Thin Slices of Behavior as Cues of Personality and Intelligence," *Journal of Personality and Social Psychology* 86, no. 4 (2014): 599–614.

Notes

41. B. Kurdi, A. E. Seitchik, J. R. Axt, T. J. Carroll, A. Karapetyan, N. Kaushik, D. Tomezsko, A. G. Greenwald, and M. R. Banaji, "Relationship Between the Implicit Association Test and Intergroup Behavior: A Meta-Analysis," *American Psychologist* 74, no. 5 (2019): 569–586.

42. F. Gino and K. Coffman, "Unconscious Bias Training That Works," *Harvard Business Review*, September–October 2021, https://hbr.org/2021/09/unconscious-bias-training-that-works.

43. D. M. Wegner, D. J. Schneider, S. R. Carter, and T. L. White, "Paradoxical Effects of Thought Suppression," *Journal of Personality and Social Psychology* 53, no. 1 (1987): 5–13.

44. J. Sinram, "'I Am Not a Racist, but . . . ,'" in *Fortress Europe? Challenges and Failures of Migration and Asylum Policies*, eds. Annette Jünemann, Nikolas Scherer, Nicolas Fromm (Wiesbaden, DE: Springer VS, 2017), 159–165.

45. M. L. Slepian and E. W. Carr, "Facial Expressions of Authenticity: Emotion Variability Increases Judgments of Trustworthiness and Leadership," *Cognition* 183 (2019): 82–98.

46. G. R. Carroll and B. Kovács, "Authenticity: Meanings, Targets, Audiences and Third Parties," *Research in Organizational Behavior* 41, no. 8 (2021), https://doi.org/10.1016/j.riob.2021.100149.

47. B. S. Connelly and S. T. Mcabee, "Reputations at Work: Origins and Outcomes of Shared Person Perceptions," *Annual Review of Organizational Psychology and Organizational Behavior* 11, no. 1 (2024): 251–278.

48. Y. Tang, E. Xu, X. Huang, and X. Pu, "When Can Display of Authenticity at Work Facilitate Coworker Interactions? The Moderating Effect of Perception of Organizational Politics," *Human Relations* 76, no. 1 (2023): 27–52.

49. S. Liu, P. Liu, M. Wang, and B. Zhang, "Effectiveness of Stereotype Threat Interventions: A Meta-Analytic Review," *Journal of Applied Psychology* 106, no. 6 (2020): 921–949.

50. I. Thielmann and B. E. Hilbig, "The Traits One Can Trust: Dissecting Reciprocity and Kindness as Determinants of Trustworthy Behavior," *Personality and Social Psychology Bulletin* 41, no. 11 (2015): 1523–1536.

51. T. Chamorro-Premuzic and A. Bhaduri, "How Office Politics Corrupt the Search for High-Potential Employees," *Harvard Business Review*, October 19, 2017, https://hbr.org/2017/10/how-office-politics-corrupt-the-search-for-high-potential-employees.

52. T. Chamorro-Premuzic, "Could Your Personality Derail Your Career?" *Harvard Business Review*, September–October 2017, https://hbr.org/2017/09/could-your-personality-derail-your-career.

53. D. S. Berry, J. W. Pennebaker, J. S. Mueller, and W. S. Hiller, "Linguistic Bases of Social Perception," *Personality and Social Psychology Bulletin* 23, no. 5 (1997): 526–537.

54. R. Hogan, J. Hogan, and B. W. Roberts, "Personality Measurement and Employment Decisions Questions and Answers," *American Psychologist* 51, no. 5 (1996): 469–477.

Chapter 5

1. N. L. Chhabra and A. Mishra, "Talent Management and Employer Branding: Retention Battle Strategies," *ICFAI Journal of Management Research* 7, no. 11 (2008): 50–61.

2. R. J. Erickson and C. Ritter, "Emotional Labor, Burnout, and Inauthenticity: Does Gender Matter?" *Social Psychology Quarterly* 64, no. 2 (2001): 146–163.

3. "How Americans View Their Jobs," Pew Research Center, March 29, 2023, https://www.pewresearch.org/social-trends/2023/03/30/how-americans-view-their-jobs/st_2023-03-30_culture-of-work_0-02-png.

4. I. Čukić and T. C. Bates, "Openness to Experience and Aesthetic Chills: Links to Heart Rate Sympathetic Activity," *Personality and Individual Differences* 64 (2014): 152–156.

5. H. M. Weiss and A. P. Brief, "Affect at Work: A Historical Perspective," in *Emotions at Work: Theory, Research and Applications in Management*, eds. Roy L. Payne and Gary L. Cooper (West Sussex: John Wiley & Sons, 2001), 133–171.

6. A. Skatova, R. McDonald, S. Ma, and C. Maple, "Unpacking Privacy: Valuation of Personal Data Protection," *PLoS One* 18, no. 5 (2023), https://doi.org/10.1371/journal.pone.0284581.

7. P. Thapa, "The Rise of Web 2.0 and Digital Narcissism: Rethinking the Aesthetics of Death," *Outlook: Journal of English Studies* 14 (2023): 33–45.

8. J. S. Michel, M. A. Clark, and D. Jaramillo, "The Role of the Five Factor Model of Personality in the Perceptions of Negative and Positive Forms of Work-Nonwork Spillover: A Meta-Analytic Review," *Journal of Vocational Behavior* 79, no. 1 (2011): 191–203.

9. E.-S. Lee and B. Koo, "Identifying Organizational Identification as a Basis for Attitudes and Behaviors: A Meta-Analytic Review," *Psychological Bulletin* 141, no. 5 (2015): 1049–1080.

10. G. Ahmetoglu, V. Swami, and T. Chamorro-Premuzic, "The Relationship Between Dimensions of Love, Personality, and Relationship Length," *Archives of Sexual Behavior* 39, no. 5 (2010): 1181–1190.

11. J. Damore, "Google's Ideological Echo Chamber" (memo, July 2017), https://www.documentcloud.org/documents/3914586-Googles-Ideological-Echo-Chamber.

12. J. D. Rose, "Diverse Perspectives on the Groupthink Theory—A Literary Review," *Emerging Leadership Journeys* 4, no. 1 (2011): 37–57.

Chapter 6

1. T. W. H. Ng, L. T. Eby, K. L. Sorensen, and D. C. Feldman, "Predictors of Objective and Subjective Career Success: A Meta-Analysis," *Personnel Psychology* 58, no. 2 (2005): 367–408.

2. Tomas Chamorro-Premuzic and Andrew Furnham, *The Psychology of Personnel Selection* (Cambridge: Cambridge University Press, 2010).

3. T. Chamorro-Premuzic, S. Adler, and R. B. Kaiser, "What Science Says About Identifying High-Potential Employees," *Harvard Business Review*, October 3, 2017, https://hbr.org/2017/10/what-science-says-about-identifying-high-potential-employees.

4. T. Chamorro-Premuzic and B. Waber, "Toward Fairer Data-Driven Performance Management," *Harvard Business Review*, December 14, 2022, https://hbr.org/2022/12/toward-fairer-data-driven-performance-management.

5. J. M. Crant and T. S. Bateman, "Assignment of Credit and Blame for Performance Outcomes," *Academy of Management Journal* 36, no. 1 (1993): 7–27.

6. Franziska Leutner, Reece Akhtar, and Tomas Chamorro-Premuzic, *The Future of Recruitment* (Bingley, UK: Emerald Publishing Limited, 2022).

7. R. Hogan and T. Chamorro-Premuzic, "Personality and Career Success," in *APA Handbook of Personality and Social Psychology: Vol. 4. Personality Processes and Individual Differences*, eds. Mario Mikulincer, Phillip R. Shaver, M. Lynne Cooper, and Randy J. Larsen (Washington, DC: American Psychological Association, 2015), 619–638.

8. F. L. Schmidt and J. E. Hunter, "The Validity and Utility of Selection Methods in Personnel Psychology: Practical and Theoretical Implications of 85 Years of Research Findings," *Psychological Bulletin* 124, no. 2 (1998): 262–274.

9. R. O. B. Silzer and A. H. Church, "The Pearls and Perils of Identifying Potential," *Industrial and Organizational Psychology* 2, no. 4 (2009): 377–412.

10. M. London, V. I. Sessa, and L. A. Shelley, "Developing Self-Awareness: Learning Processes for Self-and Interpersonal Growth," *Annual Review of Organizational Psychology and Organizational Behavior* 10 (2023): 261–288.

11. A. Morin, "Self-Awareness Part 1: Definition, Measures, Effects, Functions, and Antecedents," *Social and Personality Psychology Compass* 5, no. 10 (2011): 807–823.

12. D. L. Joseph and D. A. Newman, "Emotional Intelligence: An Integrative Meta-Analysis and Cascading Model," *Journal of Applied Psychology* 95, no. 1 (2010): 54–78.

13. "Henry Ford's Secret to Success," Ozan Varol, February 6, 2018, https://ozanvarol.com/henry-fords-secret-success.

14. D. Minor and M. G. Housman, "Toxic Workers," *Academy of Management Proceedings* 2015, no. 1 (2015): 13189.

15. T. Chamorro-Premuzic, "The Power of Leadership Humility in the AI Era," *Leader to Leader* 2024, no. 111 (2024), https://doi.org/10.1002/ltl.20777.

16. J. A. Chandler, N. E. Johnson, S. L. Jordan, D. K. B, and J. C. Short, "A Meta-Analysis of Humble Leadership: Reviewing Individual, Team, and Organizational Outcomes of Leader Humility," *Leadership Quarterly* 34, no. 1 (2023), https://doi.org/10.1016/j.leaqua.2022.101660.

17. Tomas Chamorro-Premuzic, *Why Do So Many Incompetent Men Become Leaders? (and How to Fix It)* (Brighton, MA: Harvard Business School Press, 2019); Y. Luo, Z. Zhang, Q. Chen, K. Zhang, Y. Wang, and J. Peng, "Humble Leadership and Its Outcomes: A Meta-Analysis," *Frontiers in Psychology* 13 (2022), https://doi.org/10.3389/fpsyg.2022.980322.

18. G. Blickle, C. Diekmann, P. B. Schneider, Y. Kalthöfer, and J. K. Summers, "When Modesty Wins: Impression Management Through Modesty, Political Skill, and Career Success—A Two-Study Investigation," *European Journal of Work and Organizational Psychology* 21, no. 6 (2012): 899–922.

19. A. B. van Zant, "Strategically Overconfident (to a Fault): How Self-Promotion Motivates Advisor Confidence," *Journal of Applied Psychology* 107, no. 1 (2022): 109–129.

20. I.-S. Oh, G. Wang, and M. K. Mount, "Validity of Observer Ratings of the Five-Factor Model of Personality Traits: A Meta-Analysis," *Journal of Applied Psychology* 96, no. 4 (2011): 762–773.

21. R. W. Eichinger and M. M. Lombardo, "Knowledge Summary Series: 360-Degree Assessment," *Human Resource Planning* 26 (2003): 34–45.

22. P. Babiak, C. S. Neumann, and R. D. Hare, "Corporate Psychopathy: Talking the Walk," *Behavioral Sciences and the Law* 28, no. 2 (2010): 174–193.

Chapter 7

1. J. Pfeffer, *Leadership BS: Fixing Workplaces and Careers One Truth at a Time.* (New York: Harper Business, 2015).

2. J. A. Peck and M. Hogue, "Acting with the Best of Intentions . . . or Not: A Typology and Model of Impression Management in Leadership," *Leadership Quarterly* 29, no .1 (2018): 123–134.

3. S. Côté, P. N. Lopes, P. Salovey, and C. T. H. Miners, "Emotional Intelligence and Leadership Emergence in Small Groups," *Leadership Quarterly* 21, no. 3 (2010): 496–508.

4. M. van Vugt, R. Hogan, and R. B. Kaiser, "Leadership, Followership, and Evolution: Some Lessons from the Past," *American Psychologist* 63, no. 3 (2008): 182–196.

5. A. Y. Lee-Chai and J. Bargh. *The Use and Abuse of Power* (New York: Psychology Press, 2001).

6. B. Kellerman, "How Bad Leadership Happens," *Leader to Leader* 2005, no. 35 (2005): 41–46.

7. C. S. Burke, D. E. Sims, E. H. Lazzara, and E. Salas, "Trust in Leadership: A Multi-Level Review and Integration," *Leadership Quarterly* 18, no. 6 (2007): 606–632.

8. T. Chamorro-Premuzic, "How to Tell Leaders They're Not as Great as They Think They Are," *Harvard Business Review*, March 29, 2017, https://hbr.org/2017/03/how-to-tell-leaders-theyre-not-as-great-as-they-think-they-are.

9. B. C. Gentile, J. D. Miller, B. J. Hoffman, D. E. Reidy, A. Zeichner, and W. K. Campbell, "A Test of Two Brief Measures of Grandiose Narcissism: The Narcissistic Personality Inventory-13 and the Narcissistic Personality Inventory-16," *Psychological Assessment* 25, no. 4 (2013): 1120–1136.

10. S. A. Rosenthal and T. L. Pittinsky, "Narcissistic Leadership," *Leadership Quarterly* 17, no. 6 (2006): 617–633.

11. E. Ronningstam and A. R. Baskin-Sommers, "Fear and Decision-Making in Narcissistic Personality Disorder—A Link Between Psychoanalysis and Neuroscience," *Dialogues in Clinical Neuroscience* 15, no. 2 (2013): 191–201.

12. A. Grabo, B. R. Spisak, and M. van Vugt, "Charisma as Signal: An Evolutionary Perspective on Charismatic Leadership," *Leadership Quarterly* 28, no. 4 (2017): 473–485.

13. A. H. Eagly, "Achieving Relational Authenticity in Leadership: Does Gender Matter?" *Leadership Quarterly* 16, no. 3 (2005): 459–474.

14. "Edelman 2025 Trust Barometer," https://www.edelman.com/trust/2025/trust-barometer; Jim Harter, "U.S. Employee Engagement Inches Up Slightly After 11-Year Low," Gallup, July 26, 2024, https://www.gallup.com/workplace/647564/employee-engagement-inches-slightly-year-low.aspx.

15. P. Li, K. Yin, J. Shi, T. G. E. Damen, and T. W. Taris, "Are Bad Leaders Indeed Bad for Employees? A Meta-Analysis of Longitudinal Studies Between Destructive Leadership and Employee Outcomes," *Journal of Business Ethics* 191, no. 2 (2023): 1–15.

16. T. Chamorro-Premuzic, "5 Signs a Remote Worker Is Burning Out," *Harvard Business Review*, February 3, 2025, https://hbr.org/2025/02/5-signs-a-remote-worker-is-burning-out.

17. "Could You Answer to a Robot Boss?" World Economic Forum, November 18, 2019, https://www.weforum.org/stories/2019/11/robot-boss-artificial-intelligence-jobs.

18. H. Ibarra, "The Authenticity Paradox: Why Feeling like a Fake Can Be a Sign of Growth," *Harvard Business Review*, January–February 2015, https://hbr.org/2015/01/the-authenticity-paradox.

19. Ibarra, "The Authenticity Paradox."

20. T. Chamorro-Premuzic, "Stop Focusing on Your Strengths," January 21, 2016, HBR IdeaCast, podcast, 15:31, https://hbr.org/podcast/2016/01/stop-focusing-on-your-strengths.

21. R. B. Kaiser and D. V. Overfield, "Strengths, Strengths Overused, and Lopsided Leadership," *Consulting Psychology Journal: Practice and Research* 63, no. 2 (2011): 89–109.

22. J. W. Smither, M. London, R. Flautt, Y. Vargas, and I. Kucine, "Can Working with an Executive Coach Improve Multisource Feedback Ratings over Time? A Quasi-Experimental Field Study," *Personnel Psychology* 56, no. 1 (2003): 23–44.

23. I. Kotsou, D. Nelis, J. Grégoire, and M. Mikolajczak, "Emotional Plasticity: Conditions and Effects of Improving Emotional Competence in Adulthood," *Journal of Applied Psychology* 96, no. 4 (2011): 827–839.

Chapter 8

1. "The Inclusion Solution: The Future of Diversity for the Modern Company," MindGym, 2021, https://www.web-dev.mindgym.io/resources/whitepapers/the-inclusion-solution.

2. K. Bezrukova, C. S. Spell, J. L. Perry, and K. A. Jehn, "A Meta-Analytical Integration of over 40 Years of Research on Diversity Training Evaluation," *Psychological Bulletin* 142, no. 11 (2016): 1227–1274.

3. R. Brennaman, "Discovering and Expanding Diversity with Authenticity," *Strategic HR Review* 19, no. 3 (2020): 141–142.

4. T. Chamorro-Premuzic, "The Case for Lowering Leaders' Confidence," HR Magazine, August 15, 2019, https://www.hrmagazine.co.uk/content/features/the-case-for-lowering-leaders-confidence.

5. W. Rees, "Absolute Power Corrupts Absolutely: Cassius Dio and the Fall of the Roman Republic," in *Corruption and Integrity in Ancient Greece and Rome*, ed. Philip Bosman (Pretoria: Classical Association of South Africa, 2012), 151–168.

6. L. R. Martinez, E. N. Ruggs, N. A. Smith, K. B. Sawyer, and C. N. Thoroughgood, "The Importance of Being 'Me': The Relation Between Authentic Identity Expression and Transgender Employees' Work-Related Attitudes and Experiences," *Journal of Applied Psychology* 102, no. 2 (2017): 215–226.

7. D. V. Day, D. J. Schleicher, A. L. Unckless, and N. J. Hiller, "Self-Monitoring Personality at Work: A Meta-Analytic Investigation of Construct Validity," *Journal of Applied Psychology* 87, no. 2 (2002): 390–401.

8. D. V. Day and D. J. Schleicher, "Self-Monitoring at Work: A Motive-Based Perspective," *Journal of Personality* 74, no. 3 (2006): 685–713.

9. A. J. Marcinko, "Diversity as I Say, Not as I Do: Organizational Authenticity and Diversity Management Effectiveness" (paper presented at the 80th Annual Meeting of the Academy of Management, August 2020), https://doi:10.5465/AMBPP.2020.189.

10. J. E. H. Patterson and K. E. Ruckstuhl, "Parasite Infection and Host Group Size: A Meta-Analytical Review," *Parasitology* 140, no. 7 (2013): 1–11.

11. R. Fischer, "Origins of Values Differences: A Two-Level Analysis of Economic, Climatic and Parasite Stress Explanations in the Value Domain," *Cross-Cultural Research* 55, no. 5 (2021): 438–473.

12. L. Freeman and H. Stewart, "Toward a Harm-Based Account of Micro-aggressions," *Perspectives on Psychological Science* 16, no. 5 (2021): 1008–1023.

13. S. E. Jones, J. D. Miller, and D. R. Lynam, "Personality, Antisocial Behavior, and Aggression: A Meta-Analytic Review," *Journal of Criminal Justice* 39, no. 4 (2011): 329–337.

Notes

14. J. Zhu and B. Kleiner, "The Failure of Diversity Training," Society for Nonprofits, May–June 2000, https://www.snpo.org/members/Articles/Volume18/Issue3/V180312.pdf.

15. L. R. Glasman and D. Albarracín, "Forming Attitudes That Predict Future Behavior: A Meta-Analysis of the Attitude-Behavior Relation," *Psychological Bulletin* 132, no. 5 (2006): 778–822.

16. J. H. Langlois, L. Kalakanis, A. J. Rubenstein, A. Larson, M. Hallam, and M. Smoot, "Maxims or Myths of Beauty? A Meta-Analytic and Theoretical Review," *Psychological Bulletin* 126, no. 3 (2000): 390–423.

17. P. S. Forscher, C. Lai, J. R. Axt, C. R. Ebersole, M. Herman, P. C. Devine, and B. A. Nosek, "A Meta-Analysis of Procedures to Change Implicit Measures," *Journal of Personality and Social Psychology* 117, no. 3 (2019): 522–559.

18. R. J. Giuliano and N. Y. Y. Wicha, "Why the White Bear Is Still There: Electrophysiological Evidence for Ironic Semantic Activation During Thought Suppression," *Brain Research* 1316 (2010): 62–74.

19. M. J. Williams and L. Z. Tiedens, "The Subtle Suspension of Backlash: A Meta-Analysis of Penalties for Women's Implicit and Explicit Dominance Behavior," *Psychological Bulletin* 142, no. 2 (2016): 165–197.

20. T. W. H. Ng, S. S. K. Lam, and D. C. Feldman, "Organizational Citizenship Behavior and Counterproductive Work Behavior: Do Males and Females Differ?" *Journal of Vocational Behavior* 93 (2016): 11–32.

21. P. M. Podsakoff, S. B. MacKenzie, J. B. Paine, and D. G. Bachrach, "Organizational Citizenship Behaviors: A Critical Review of the Theoretical and Empirical Literature and Suggestions for Future Research," *Journal of Management* 26, no. 3 (2000): 513–563.

22. Natasha Bowman, "Creating a Culture of Civility," chap. 8 in *The Power of One* (New York: Productivity Press, 2022).

23. J. J. Kish-Gephart, D. A. Harrison, and L. K. Treviño, "Bad Apples, Bad Cases, and Bad Barrels: Meta-Analytic Evidence About Sources of Unethical Decisions at Work," *Journal of Applied Psychology* 95, no. 1 (2010): 1–31.

Index

costs of ignoring, 90, 105–107, 110–111
creativity and adherence to, 75–76, 82, 83–85
diluted or sweetened persona to modify, 104–112
disadvantages of too much concern for, 89–90, 99, 153, 189
diversity, inclusion, and views on, 94, 189–190, 195
emotional intelligence and, 43–44, 139–144
empathy swaying, 86–95, 104–105, 108, 112, 143
first impressions in, 100–104
of honesty, 43–44, 105, 107
importance and value of, 23–25, 76–79, 82–83, 87–90, 93, 103–112, 195, 206–212
inhibition loss and, 90–92, 153
language and communication affecting, 109–110
leadership views of, 77–78, 87, 160–161, 164, 166
myths of unimportance of, 87–88
narcissists and egoists dismissing, 9, 24, 86–87, 92, 93, 110–111, 166
neurodiversity and, 89, 92–93
non-conformity and rule-breaking as rebellion against, 75–85, 90–92, 166
overview of, 23–25, 75–79
philosophical foundations for views on, 79–85
power and dismissal of, 87, 160–161
prioritizing, 206–212
reputation and, 95–100, 101, 105–106, 108–112, 128, 189, 195, 209
self-awareness of, 80–81, 83, 95, 96–97, 107
selfishness in ignoring, 82
self-views vs., 110–111, 150–152
social capital and, 85

social learning on, 83–84, 86–87, 88–89, 102
of trustworthiness, 79, 100–102, 104, 108, 134
values, morals, and, 66, 68–74, 86, 94–95, 128, 171

Peek, Kim, 89
perception of you. See others' perceptions
Peterson, Jordan, 80
Pfeffer, Jeffrey, 159
Piaget, Jean, 86–87
Picasso, Pablo, 81, 83
Pinakothek, 96
Plato, 198
Popper, Karl, 72
positive psychology, 6, 14, 145
power, 87, 160–161, 163, 180, 198
prejudice. See discrimination, bias, and prejudice
psychological safety, 53, 178, 198–199, 202–204
psychopathy, 92, 108, 153, 166
psychosis, 16

radical freedom, 79–80
radical transparency, 50–54
rational compassion, 200–201
remote work. See work-from-home
reputation
  baselining of, 108–109
  career advancement reflecting, 134–136, 138–139, 141
  emotional intelligence effects on, 141
  of leaders, 161, 172
  others' perceptions and, 95–100, 101, 105–106, 108–112, 128, 189, 195, 209
Rivera, Diego, 77

Index

Acknowledgments

Writing a book is a lonely, slow, and occasionally masochistic pursuit—especially when it's something you do on the side, like knitting, except with more existential dread and less wool. In my case, I couldn't have done it without the help, patience, and intellectual generosity of many colleagues, students, editors, and friends who made the process slightly less isolating, much more efficient—and occasionally even fun.

Though it would take another book to properly thank everyone who contributed, a few people deserve special mention:

To Herminia Ibarra, who inspired me to rethink authenticity and has an uncanny habit of being, like Miles Davis, always miles ahead of the rest of us. Let's face it—we're all just footnotes to Herminia.

To Adrian Furnham, for reprogramming my brain to always approach questions with a healthy degree of academic (very British) skepticism, and encouraging me to disseminate common-sensical arguments that have curiously become controversial or heretical (especially in the US).

To Barbara Kellerman, for being a courageous role model on leadership, talent, and big-picture thinking in organizational science and human affairs.

To Katarina Berg, who acts as my trusted sparring partner, always ready to poke holes in my arguments—even when she sort of agrees with them. Agreeable contrarianism is an art form, just like reading between the lines.

To Amy Edmondson, my dear friend and unconditional mentor, for always encouraging me to inject science and logic into flawed popular thinking.

Acknowledgments

To my amazing ManpowerGroup colleagues—especially Becky Frankiewicz, Monica Flores, and Michelle Nettles—for helping me shape and refine my views through deep, fun, and candid discussions, and making corporate life fun.

To the editors who helped incubate early versions of these ideas into coherent thoughts: Dana Rousmaniere at *Harvard Business Review*, and Kathleen Davis and Lydia Dishman at *Fast Company*—thank you for turning rough drafts and unfiltered ruminations into something cogent and readable.

To my agent, Giles Anderson, for being simply the best, and sticking with me book after book.

To the editor of this book, Kevin Evers, for always finding a way to cope with my ideas and suggestions, no matter how unhinged or exotic, and helping me edit my authentic self.

To my students and former students at University College London and Columbia University, who helped with research and material curation, and proved over and over again that human curiosity cannot be automated.

To generative AI, for being a mostly reliable thought partner, offering examples, summaries, analogies, jokes (the good ones are mine though), and never being moody or irritable, perhaps because it isn't authentic.

And finally, to Mylène, Isabelle, and Viktor—thank you for your love, patience, and the many weekends you generously donated to this project.

About the Author

TOMAS CHAMORRO-PREMUZIC is an international authority in talent management, leadership development, executive coaching, and the human-AI interface. His commercial work focuses on the creation of science-based tools that improve organizations' ability to predict and understand human performance at work. He is currently the chief innovation officer at ManpowerGroup, co-founder of DeeperSignals and Metaprofiling, and professor of business psychology at University College London and Columbia University. He has previously held academic positions at New York University and the London School of Economics, and lectured at Harvard Business School, Stanford Business School, London Business School, Johns Hopkins, IMD, and INSEAD, as well as being the CEO at Hogan Assessment Systems.

Dr. Tomas has published 14 books and over 300 scientific papers on the psychology of talent, leadership, innovation, and AI, making him one of the most prolific social scientists of his generation. His work has received awards by the American Psychological Association, the International Society for the Study of Individual Differences, and the Society for Industrial-Organizational Psychology, to which he is a Fellow. He is also consistently ranked by Thinkers50 as one of the top thought leaders and academics on the topics of talent, leadership, and innovation. Dr. Tomas is the founding director of University College London's Industrial-Organizational and Business Psychology program, and the chief psychometric advisor to Harvard's Entrepreneurial Finance Lab.

Over the past 25 years, he has consulted to a wide range of clients in financial services (e.g., JP Morgan, HSBC, Goldman Sachs), advertising (e.g., Google, WPP, BBH), media (e.g., BBC, *The New Yorker*, Spotify), consumer goods (e.g., Unilever, PepsiCo, P&G, and Red Bull), fashion (e.g., LVMH, Net-a-Porter, Valentino, Gucci), government (e.g., British Army, Royal Mail, NHS, and Australian Defense Force), and intergovernmental organizations (e.g., United Nations, International Rescue Committee and the World Bank).

Dr. Tomas' media career comprises over 250 TV appearances, including on the BBC, CNN, Channel Four, and Sky News, and over 300 features in *Harvard Business Review*, the *Guardian*, Fast Company, *Forbes*, and the Huffington Post. Dr. Tomas is also a regular keynote speaker for the Institute of Economic Affairs, TED, and SIOP. He was born and raised in the Villa Freud district of Buenos Aires, but spent most of his professional career in London and New York. His recent books include *I, Human: AI, Automation, and the Quest to Reclaim What Makes Us Unique*, and *Why So Many Incompetent Men Become Leaders (and How to Fix It)*, both by Harvard Business Review Press. You can find him on www.drtomas.com.